AF575938

EASTERN OREGON

BARBARA TRICARICO

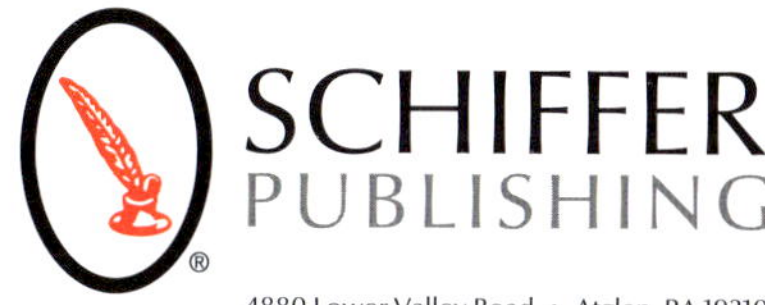

4880 Lower Valley Road • Atglen, PA 19310

Other Schiffer Books by the Author:
Oregon Coast, ISBN 978-0-7643-5947-7
Southern Oregon, ISBN 978-0-7643-5948-4
Central Oregon, ISBN 978-0-7643-5945-3

Library of Congress Control Number: 2020943523

Designed by Molly Shields
Cover design by Danielle Farmer
Front cover photo by John Kirk
Back cover photos by Vldn Taylor and Neal R. Thompson

Type set in BentonSans/Cambria

ISBN: 978-0-7643-6158-6
Printed in China

Published by Schiffer Publishing, Ltd.
4880 Lower Valley Road
Atglen, PA 19310
Phone: (610) 593-1777; Fax: (610) 593-2002
E-mail: Info@schifferbooks.com
Web: www.schifferbooks.com

INTRODUCTION

Visiting eastern Oregon is like stepping back in time. Think of the hot, dry Wild West from movies of the 1950s, with ghost and mining towns, covered wagons, free-range cattle, pronghorn, wild mustangs, and abundant tumbleweeds.

The Steens Mountain, Leslie Gulch, and Alford Desert have untouched geological formations. The Snake River has carved the deepest river gorge in North America at Hells Canyon.

The Wallowas, considered one of the Seven Wonders of Oregon, are nicknamed the Little Switzerland of America. The John Day Fossil Beds National Monument is expansive and beautiful, with three unique areas to explore. The popular Painted Hills, also considered one of the Seven Wonders of Oregon, is one of the most picturesque and often-visited areas of Eastern Oregon.

The Malheur National Wildlife Refuge, south of Burns, has approximately 320 known species of birds and fifty-eight species of mammals in the park. Located in the remote southeastern part of Oregon, Steens Mountain has a high elevation of 9,733 feet. There you'll see wild horses, sagebrush, and, nearby, the parched and isolated Alvord Desert. The Owyhee Canyonlands has only three paved roads cutting across the territory.

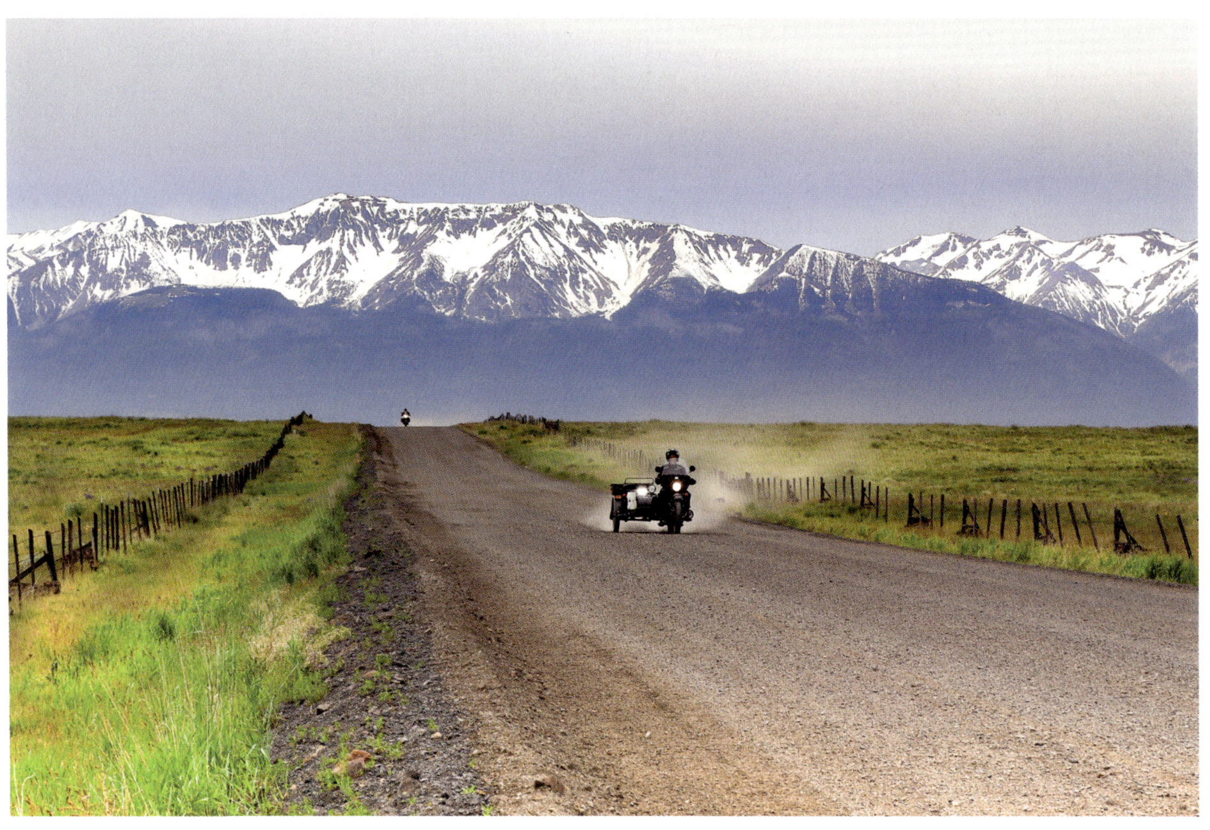

Motorcycles near the Wallowa Mountains.
Photo by Terry Fisher

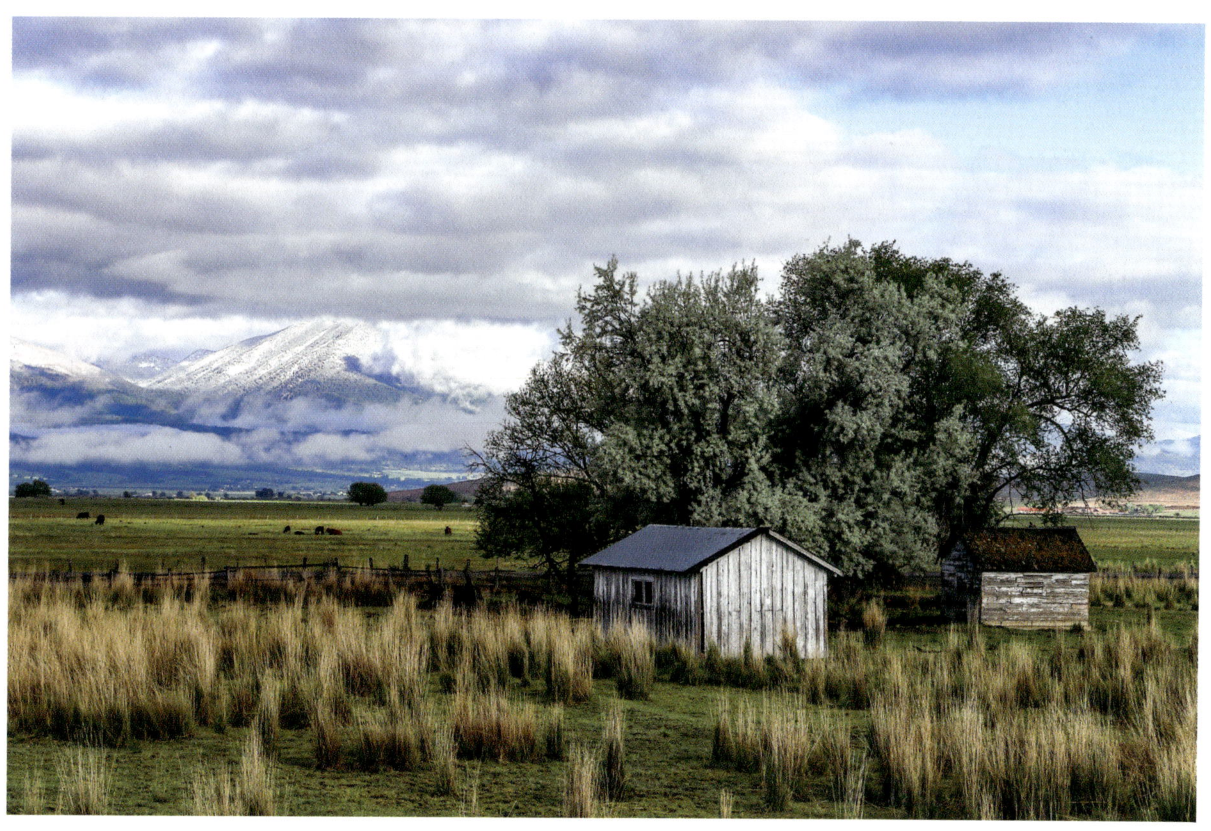

Blue Mountains. *Photo by Terry Fisher*

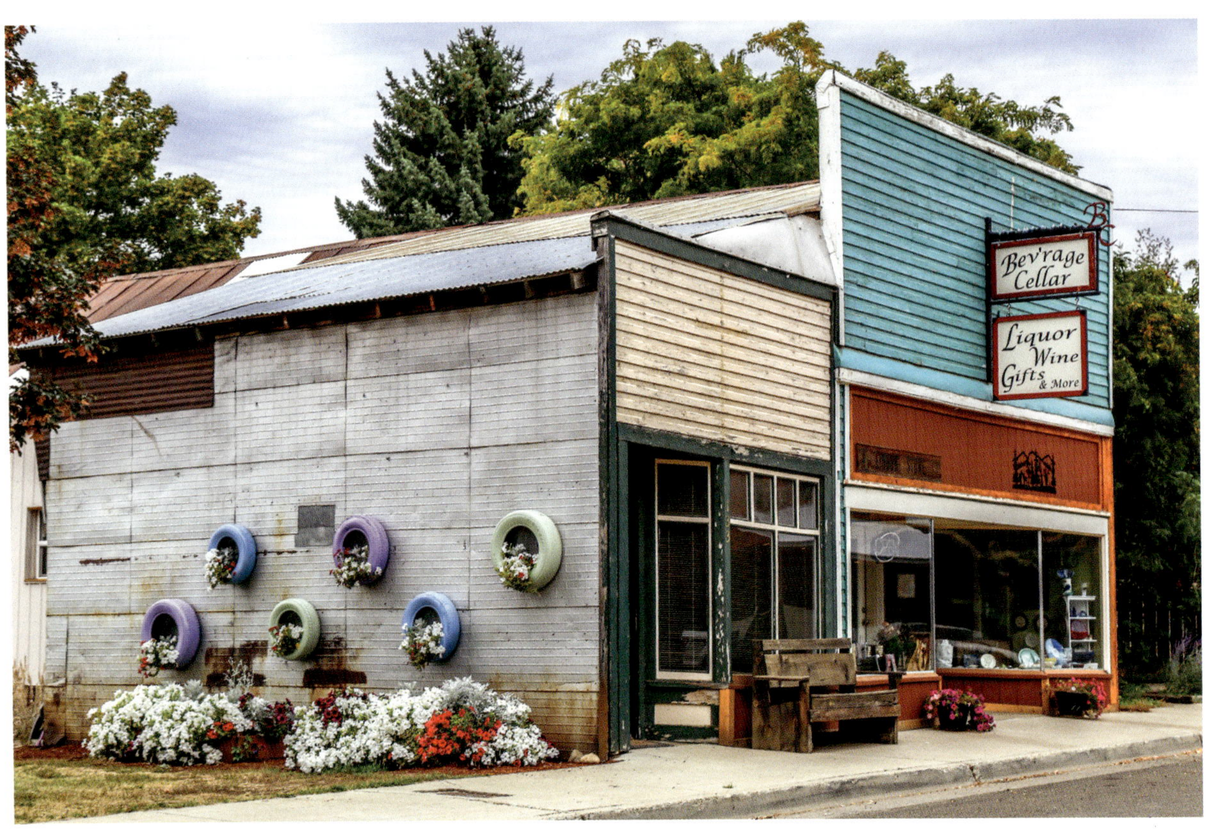

Downtown Halfway. *Photo by Terry Fisher*

Grass Valley. *Photo by Neal R. Thompson*

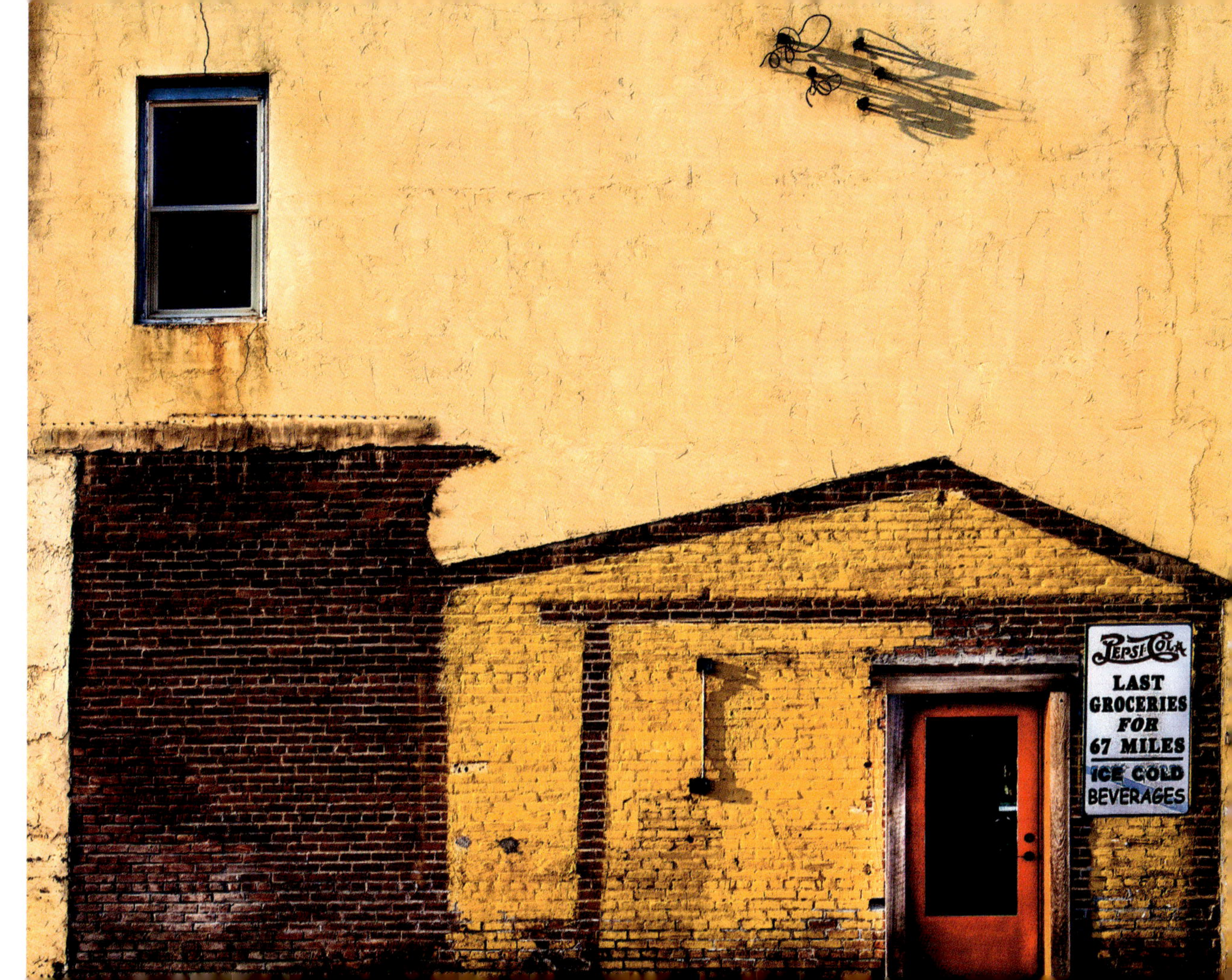
Pepsi-Cola
LAST
GROCERIES
FOR
67 MILES
ICE COLD
BEVERAGES

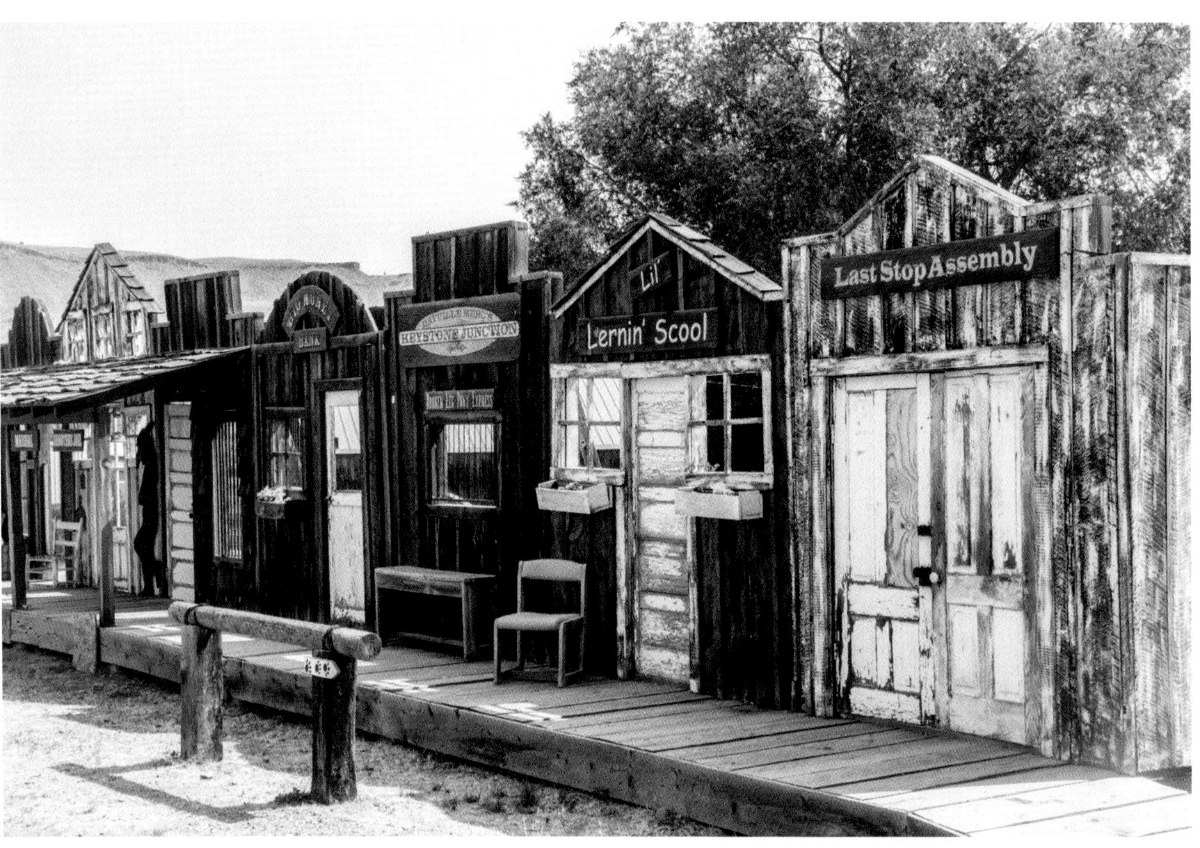

Dayville. *Photo by Diana Standing*

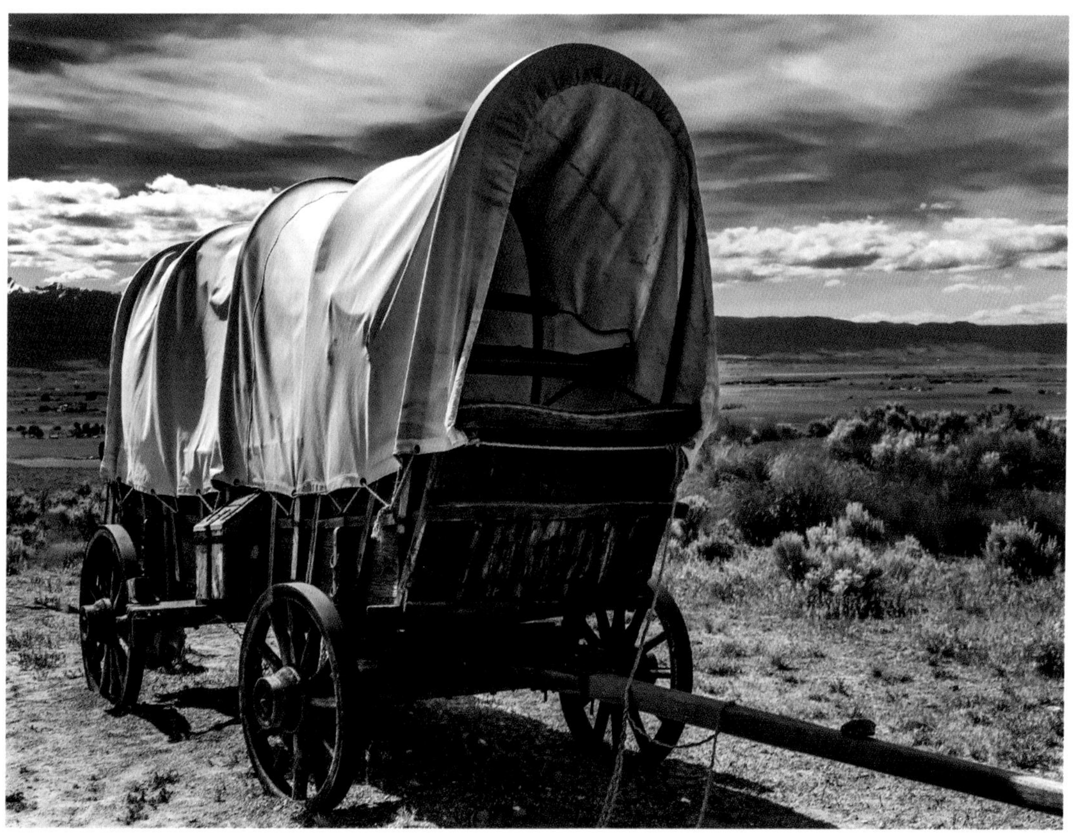

Covered wagon at the Oregon Trail Interpretive Center.
Photo by Alan Ingersoll

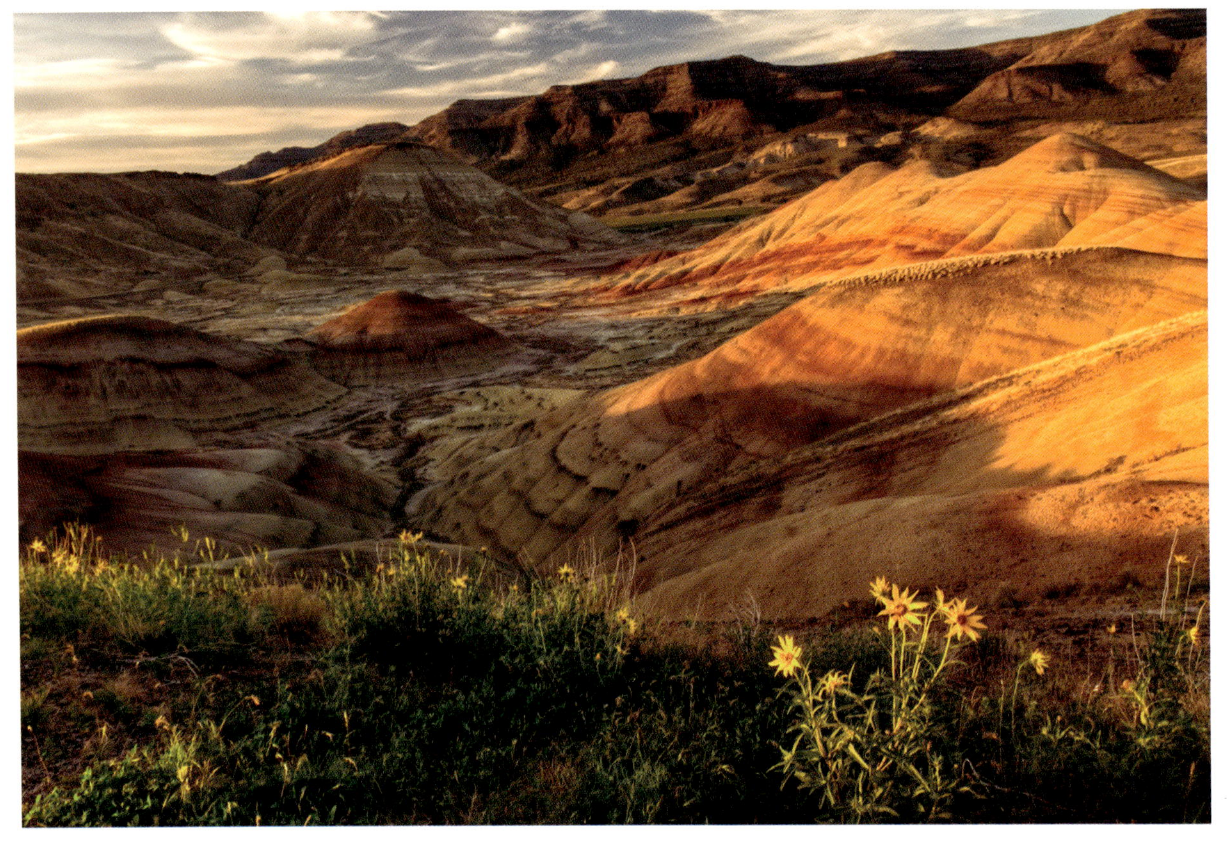

Painted Hills. *Photo by Sue Newman*

Painted Hills storm. *Photo by John Kirk*

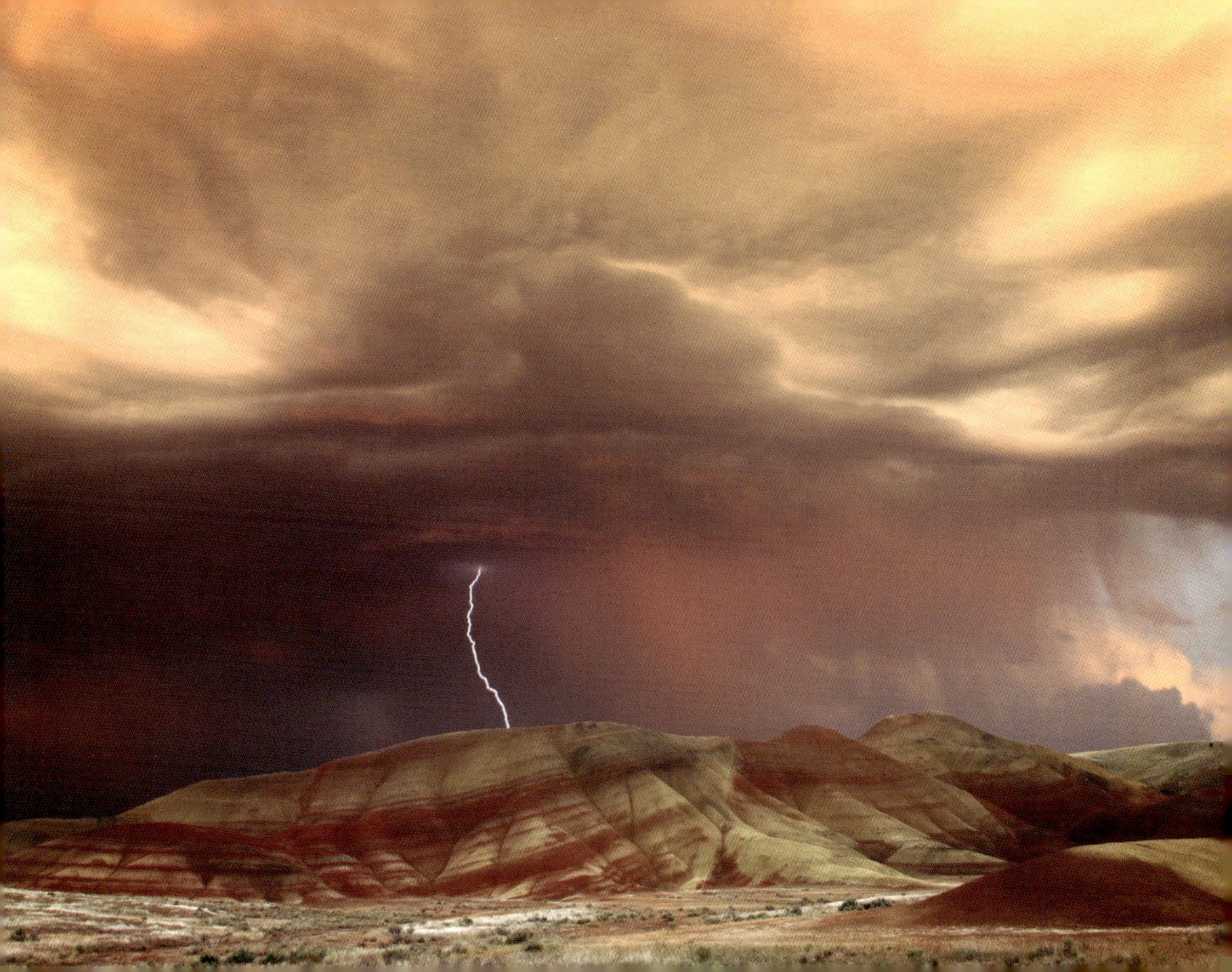

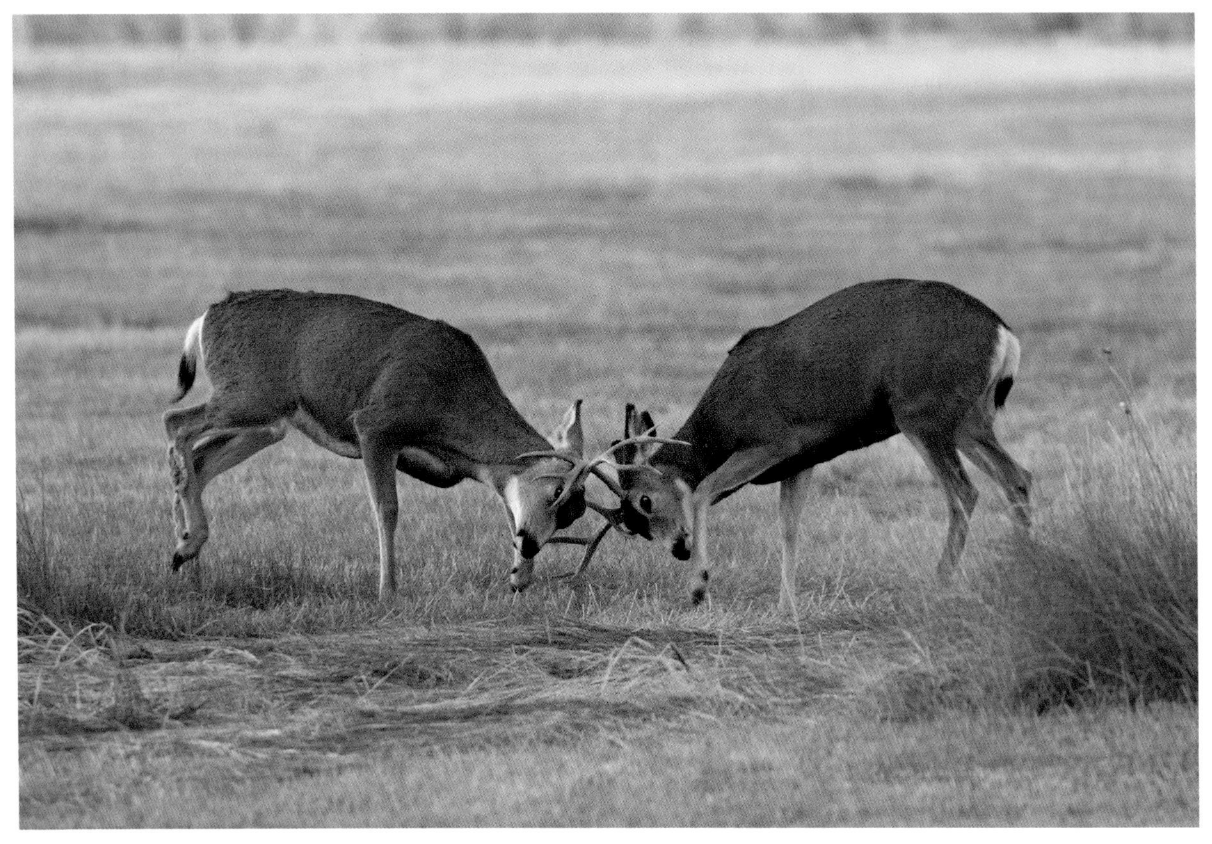

Young mule deer. *Photo by Dan Elster*

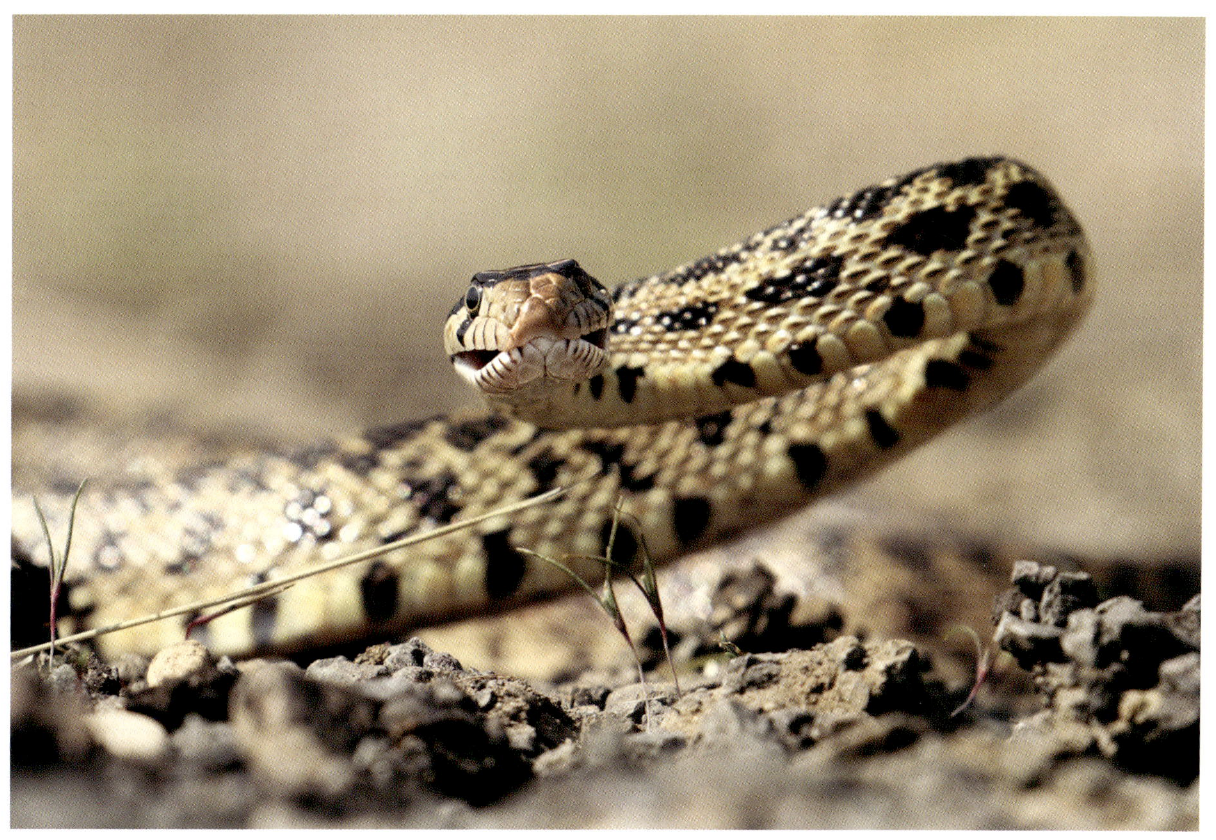

Gopher snake. *Photo by Dan Elster*

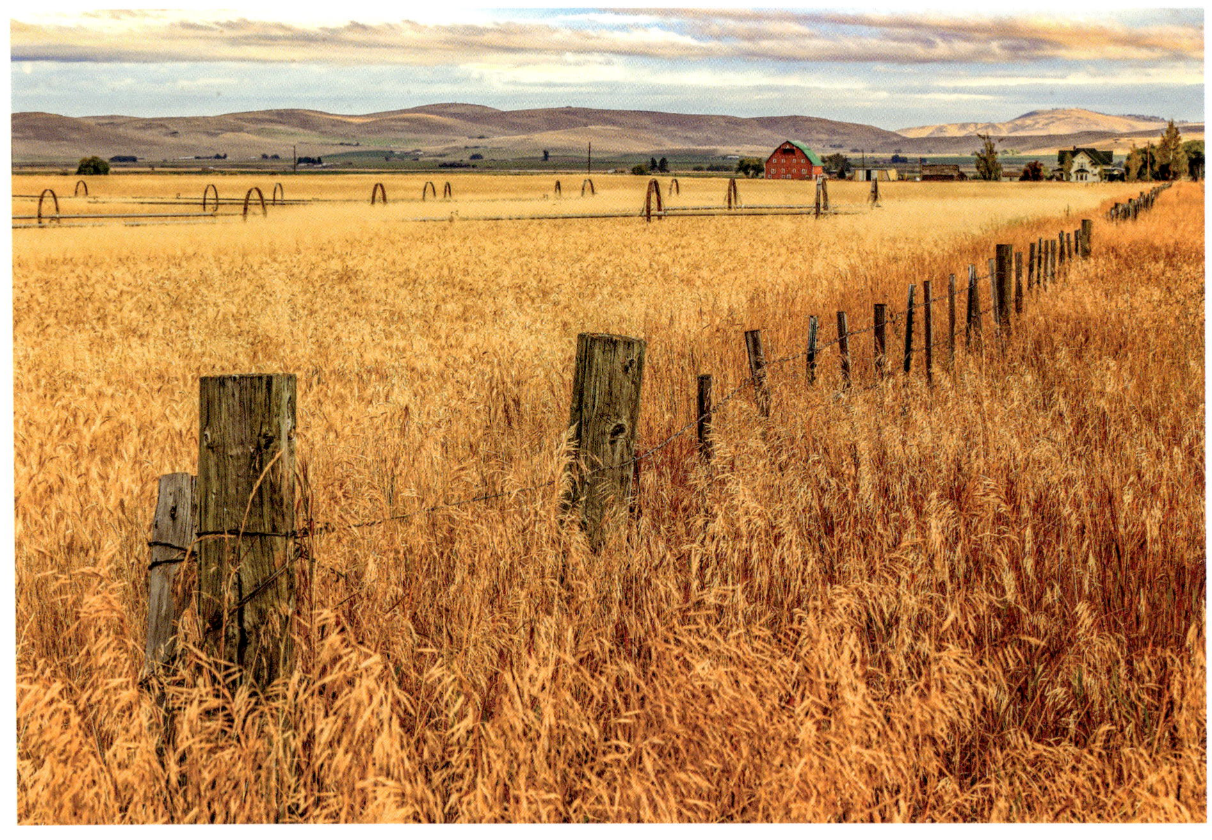

Grain farm near Joseph. *Photo by Terry Fisher*

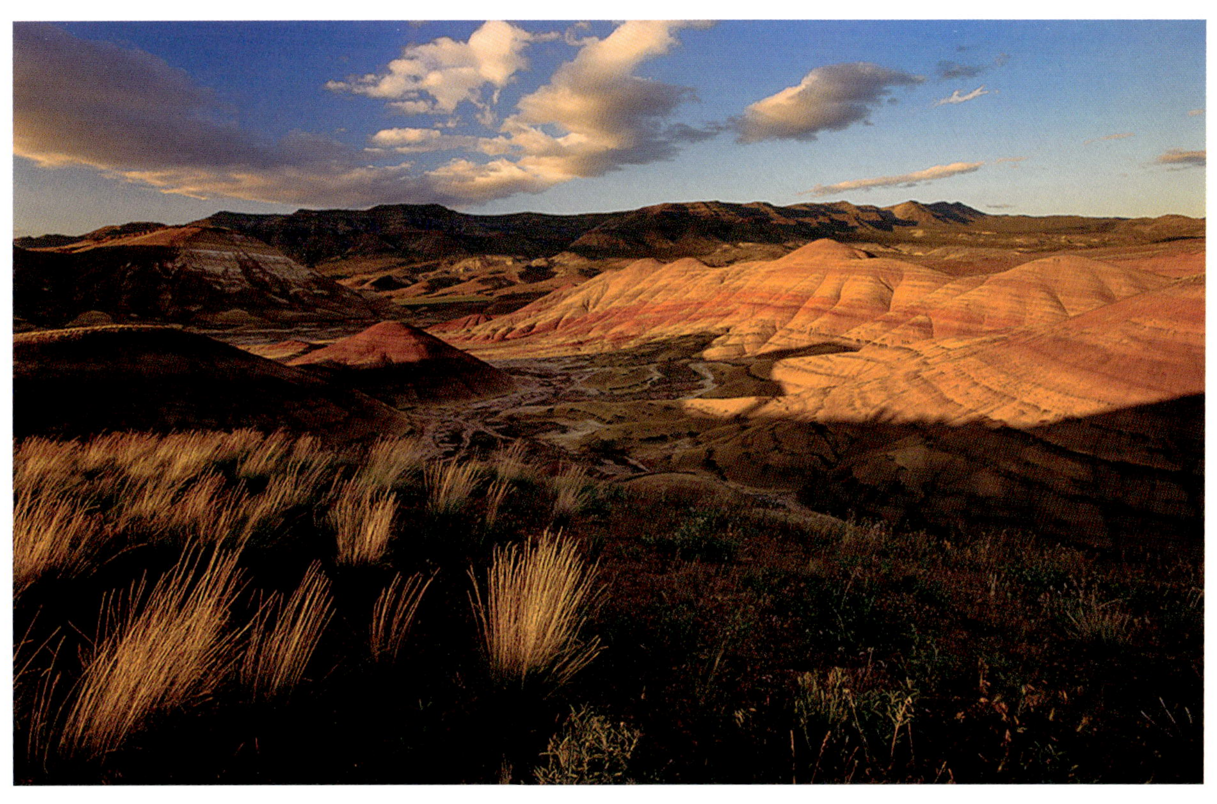

Painted Hills. *Photo by Clem Paslack*

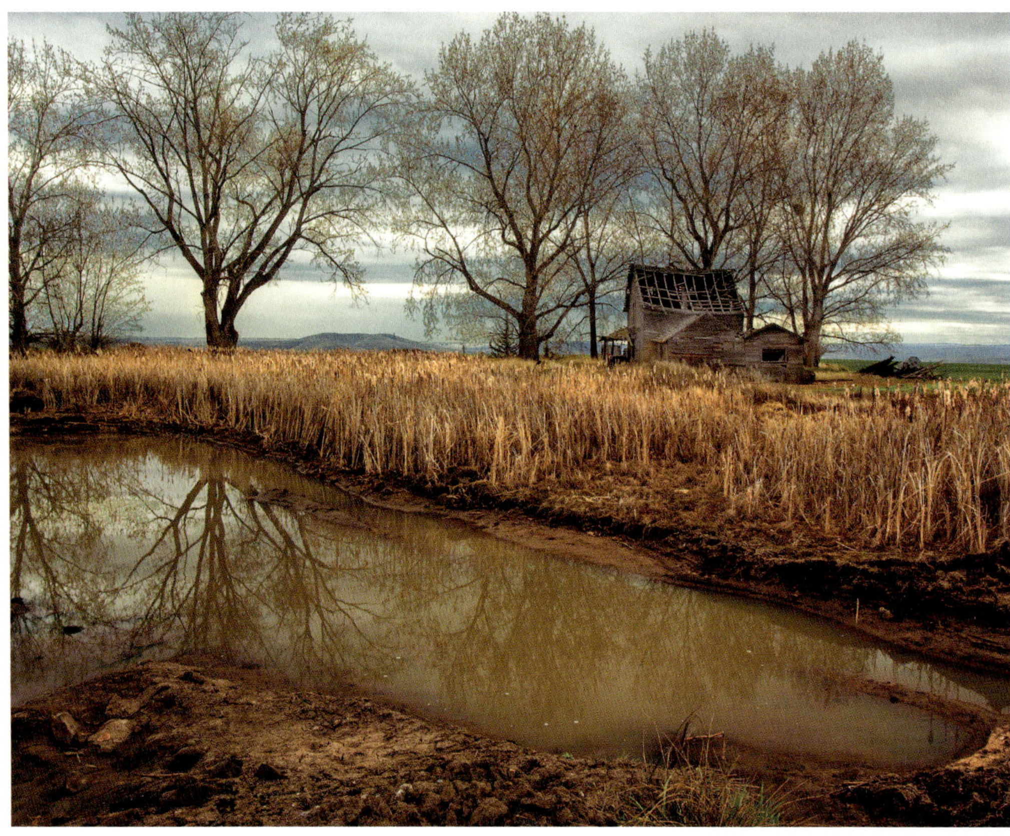

Dufur is a farming community. *Photo by Neal R. Thompson*

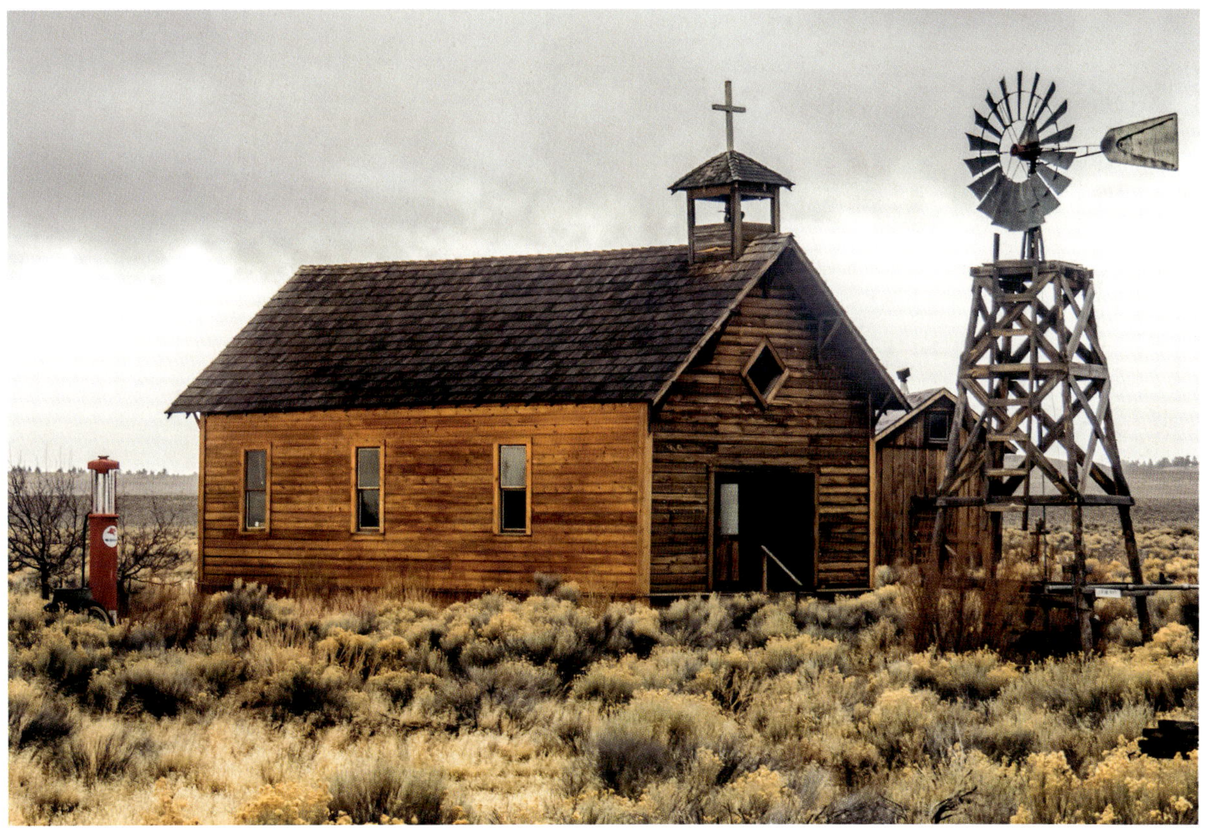

Fort Rock. The museum features a collection of historic buildings that were moved onto the grounds from remote locations in the area. *Photo by Randy Bryan*

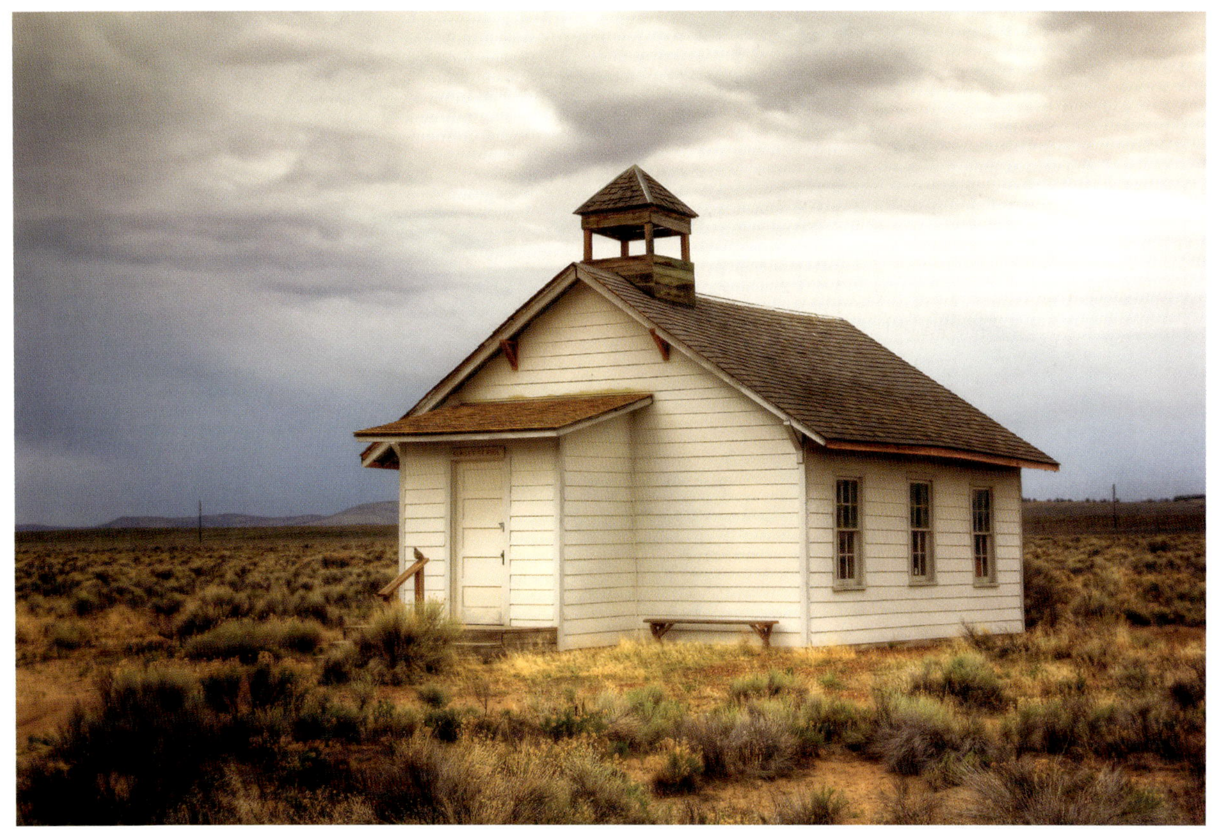

Sunset School, Fort Rock. *Photo by Nomeca Hartwell*

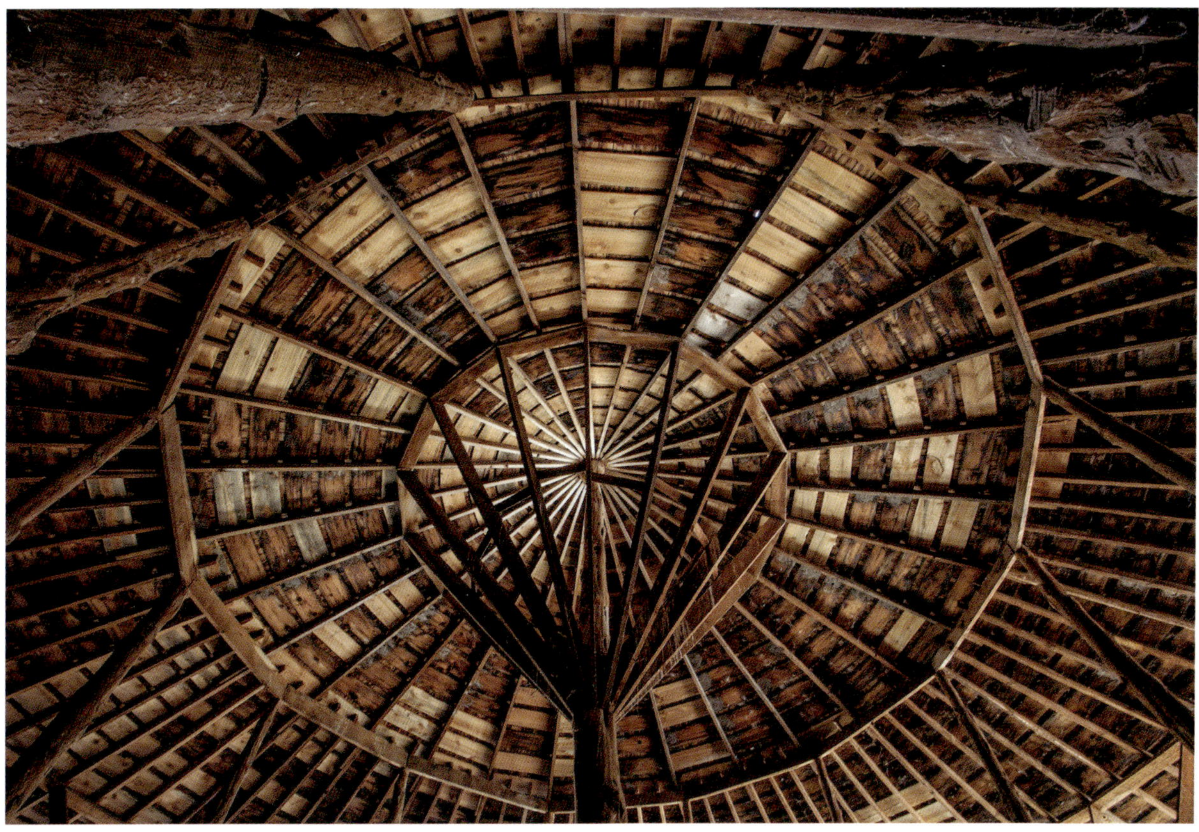

Round barn. *Photo by Neal R. Thompson*

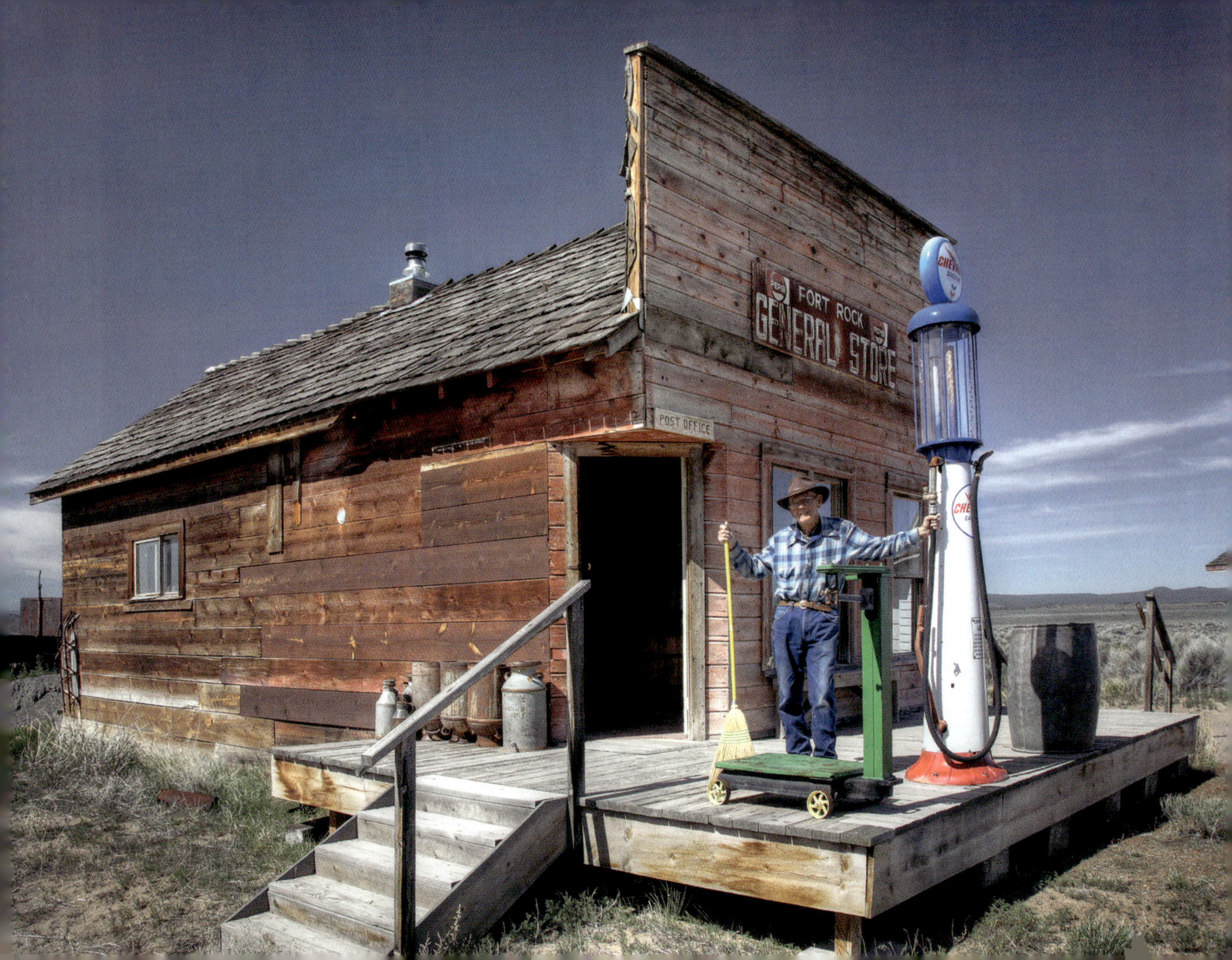
FORT ROCK
GENERAL STORE
POST OFFICE

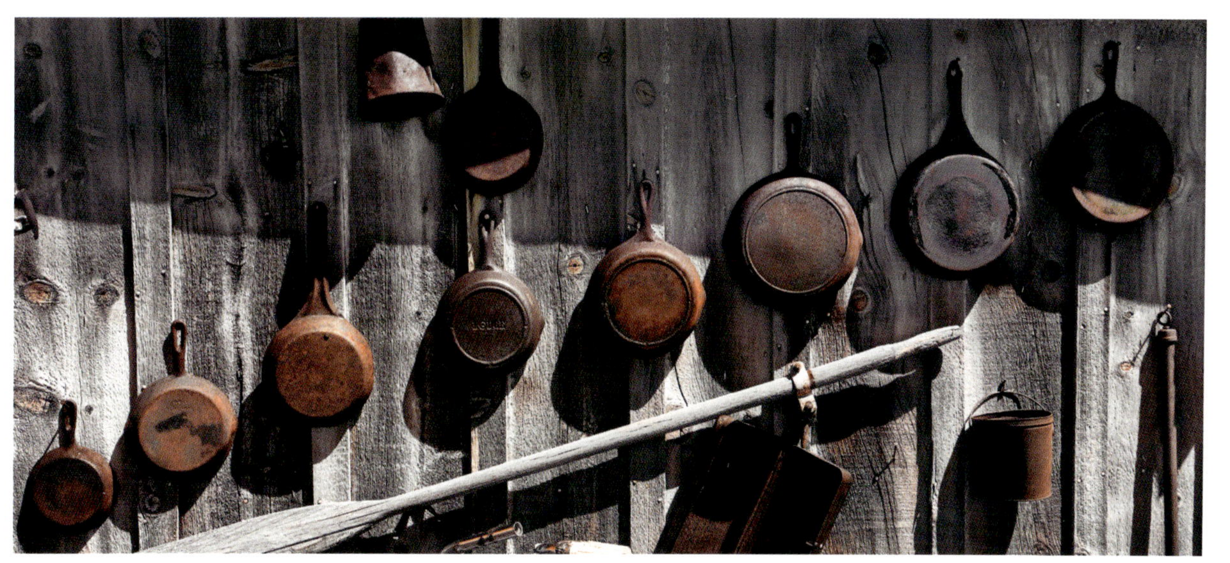

Fort Rock General Store, opened in the early 1900s.
Photo by John Kirk

Fort Rock. *Photo by John Kirk*

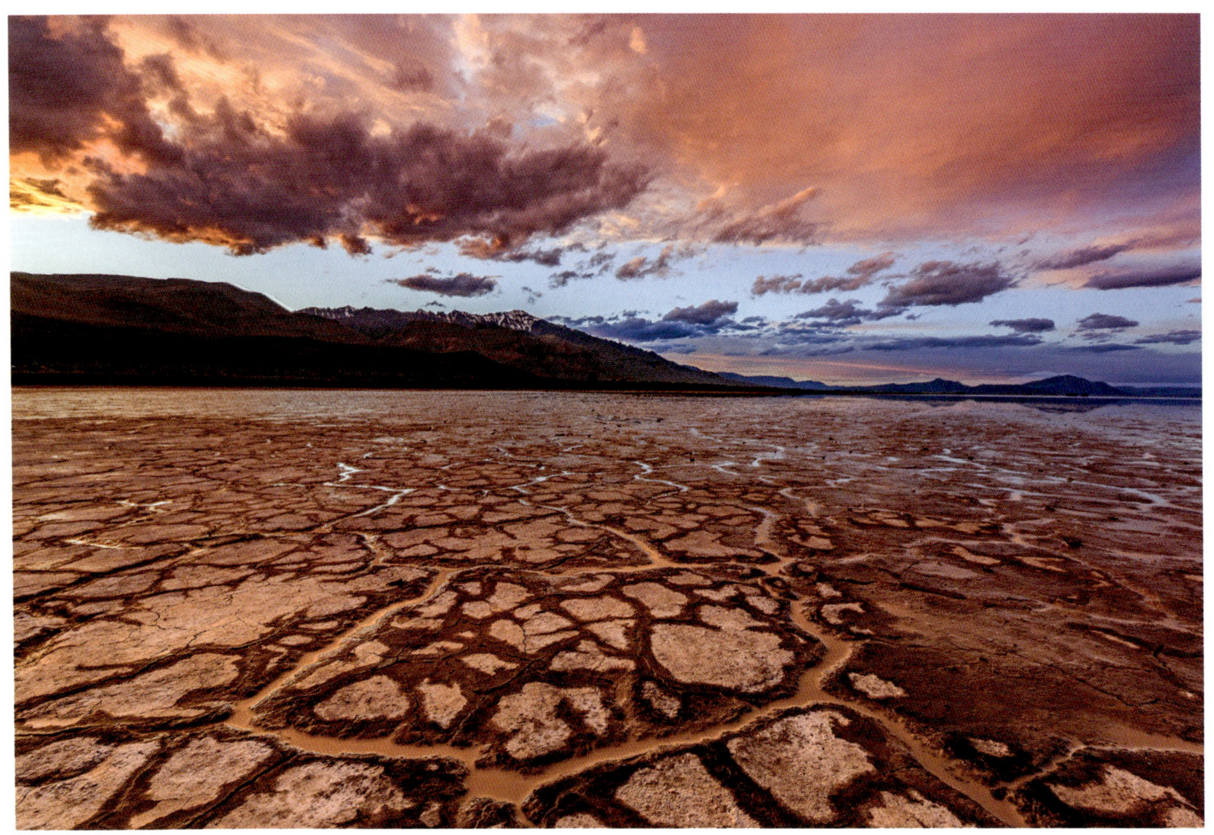

Alvord Desert. *Photo by Vldn Taylor*

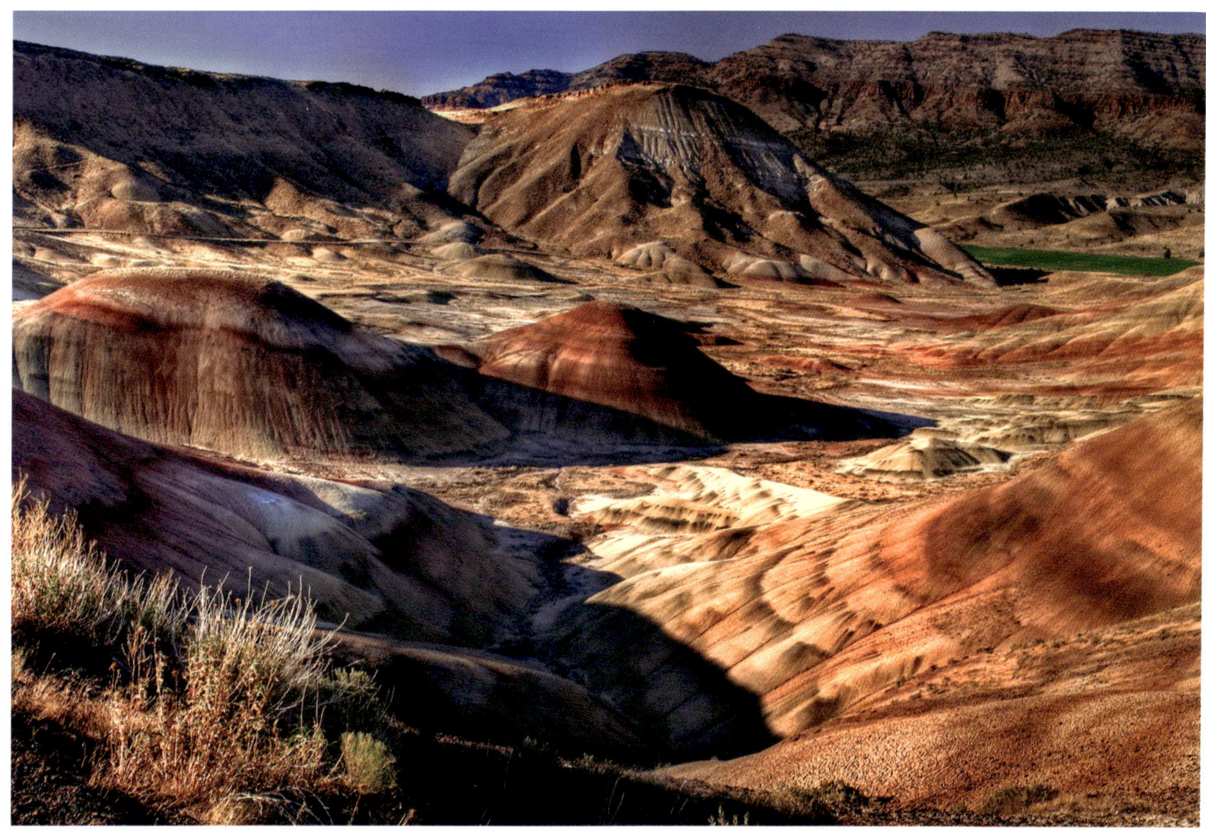

Painted Hills. *Photo by Neal R. Thompson*

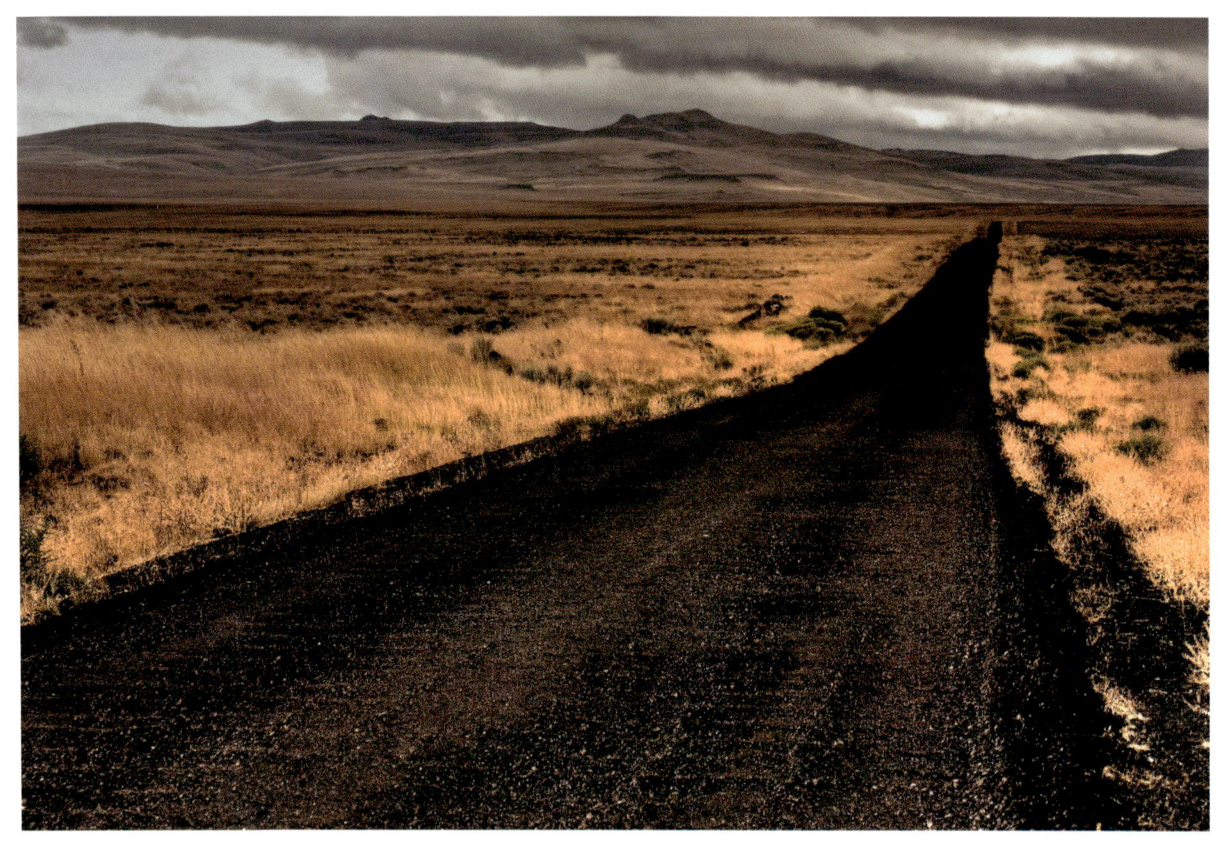

Hart Mountain. *Photo by Jay Newman*

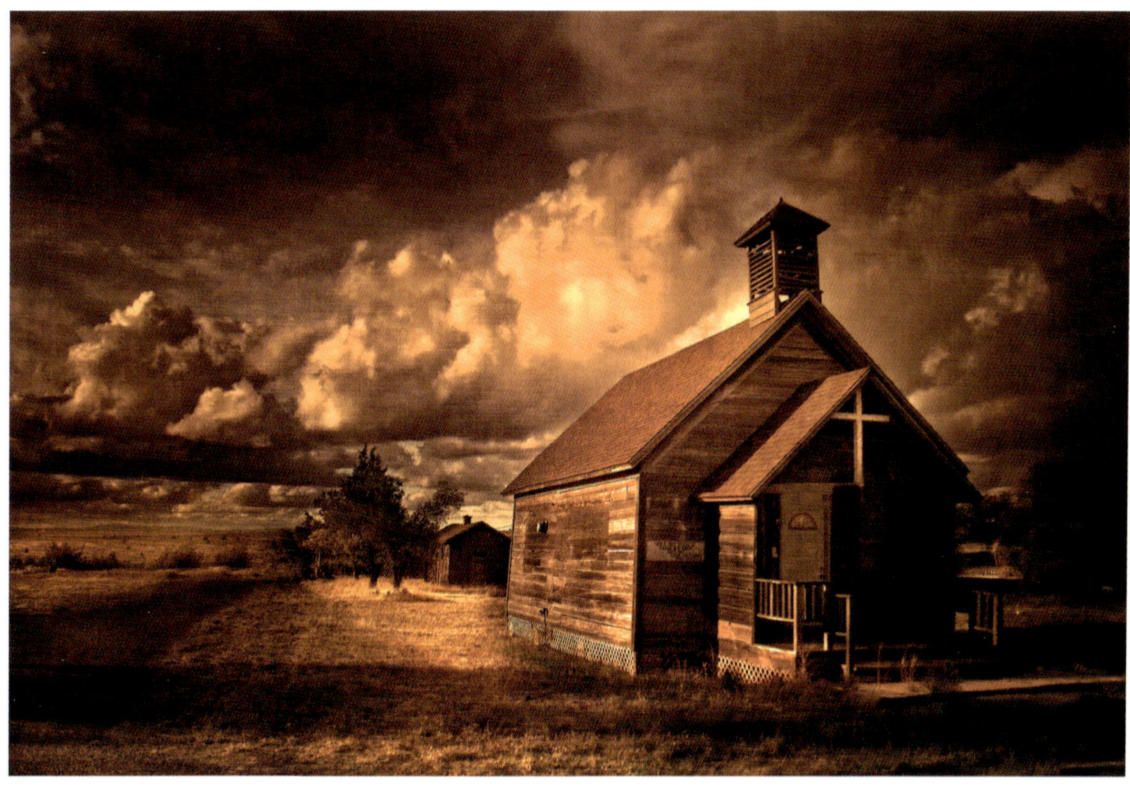

Prairie Church, Shaniko. Now almost a ghost town (population thirty-six), Shaniko was once known as Wool Capital of the World. It was named for August Scherneckau in 1879 (the spelling of Shaniko reflects the regional pronunciation of his name). *Photo by Neal R. Thompson*

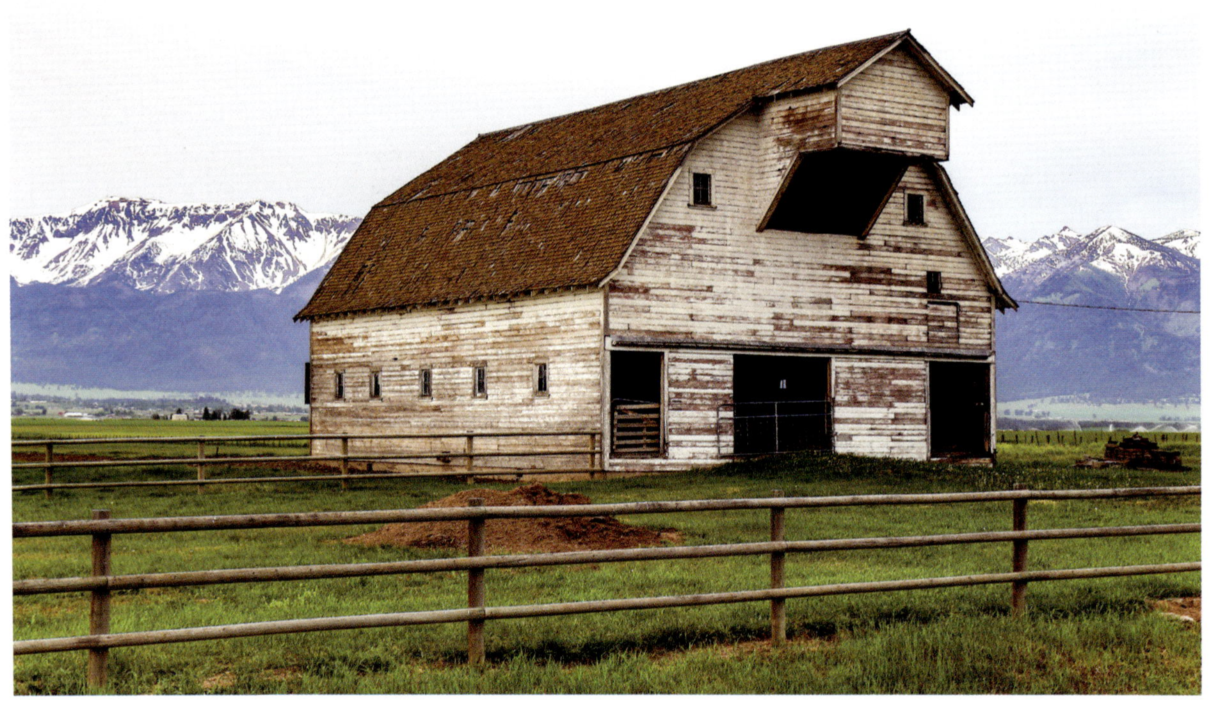

Barn in Enterprise, near the Wallowa Mountains.
Photo by Terry Fisher

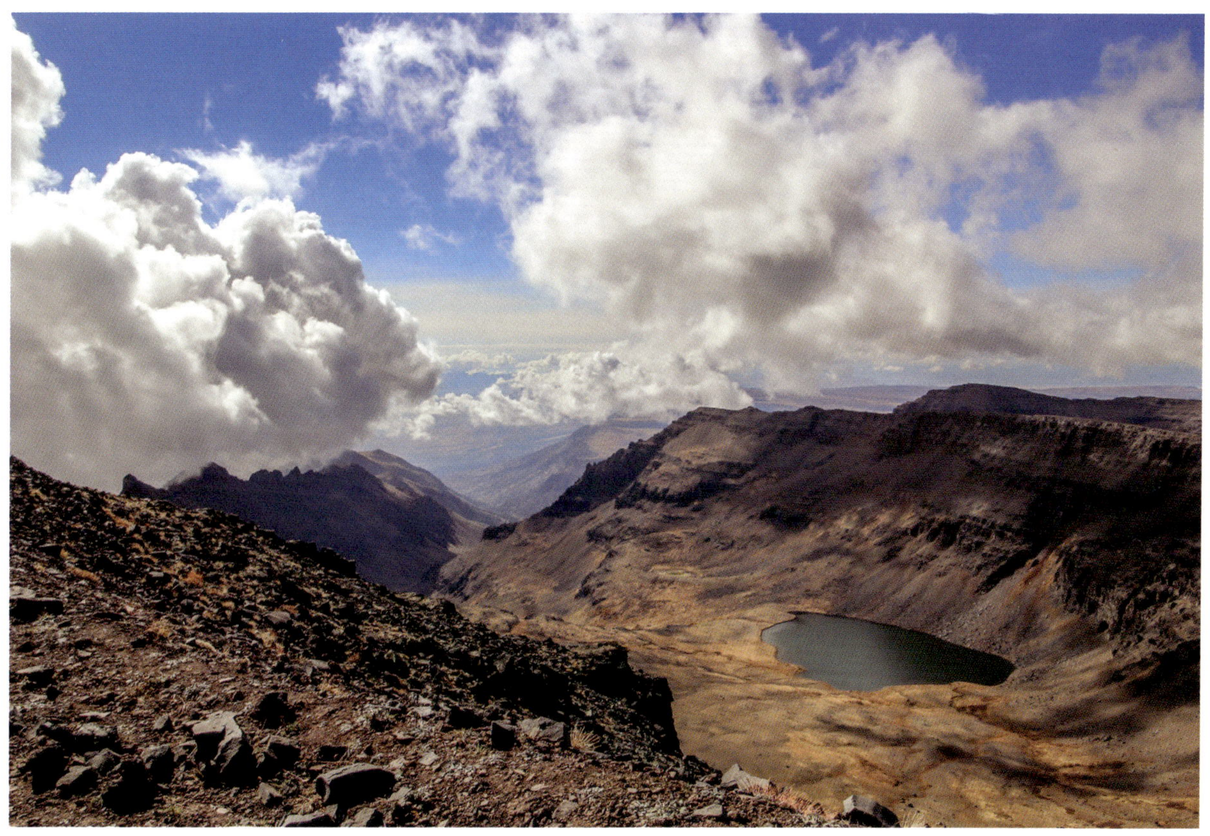

Wildhorse Lake, Steens Mountain. *Photo by Diana Standing*

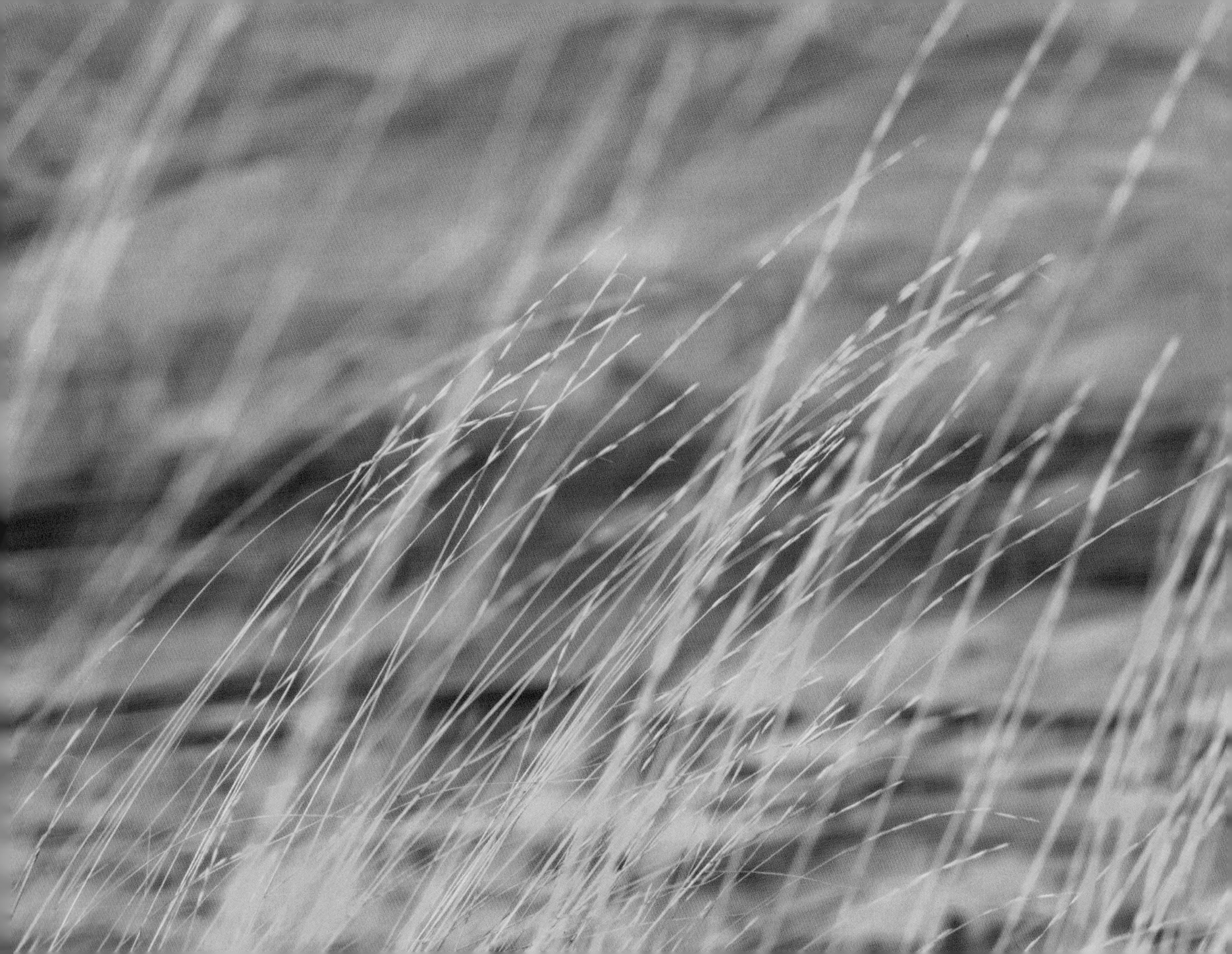

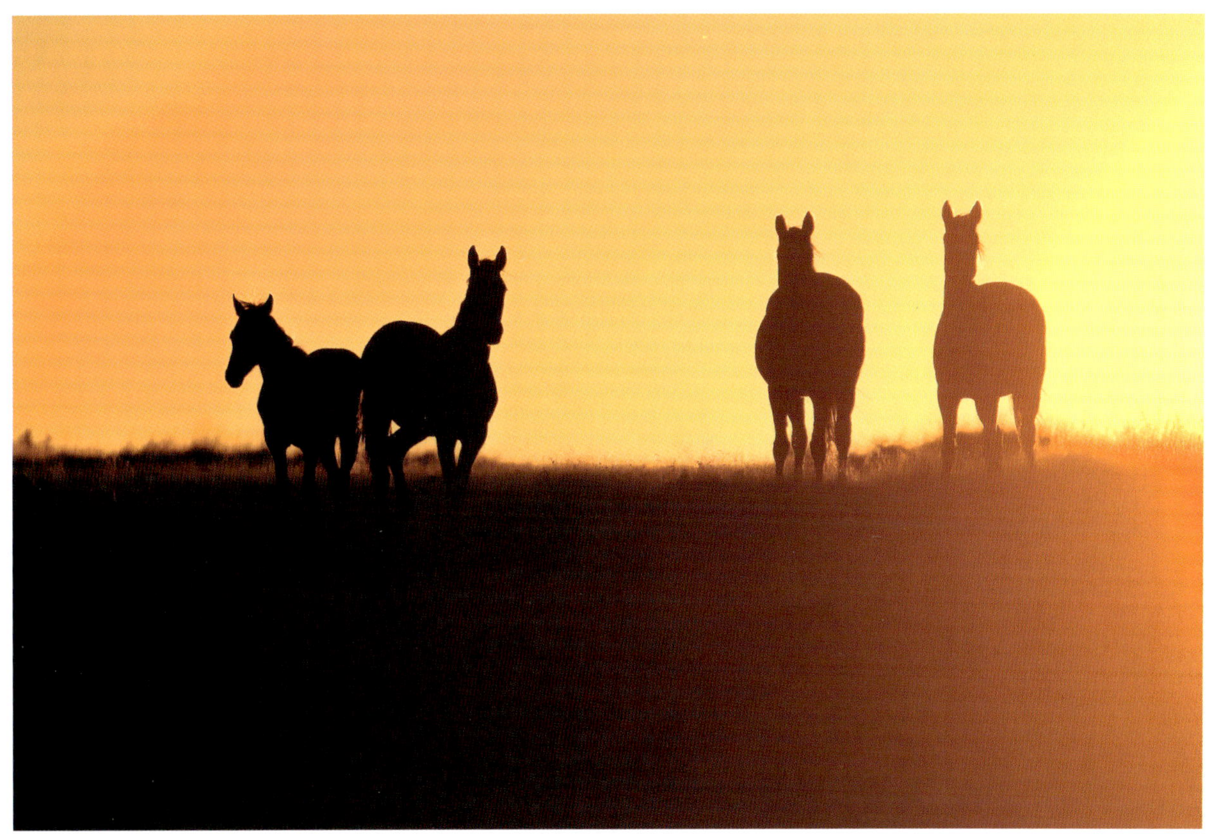

Painted Hills. *Photo by Vivian McAleavey*

Wild mustangs, Steens Mountain. *Photo by Dan Elster*

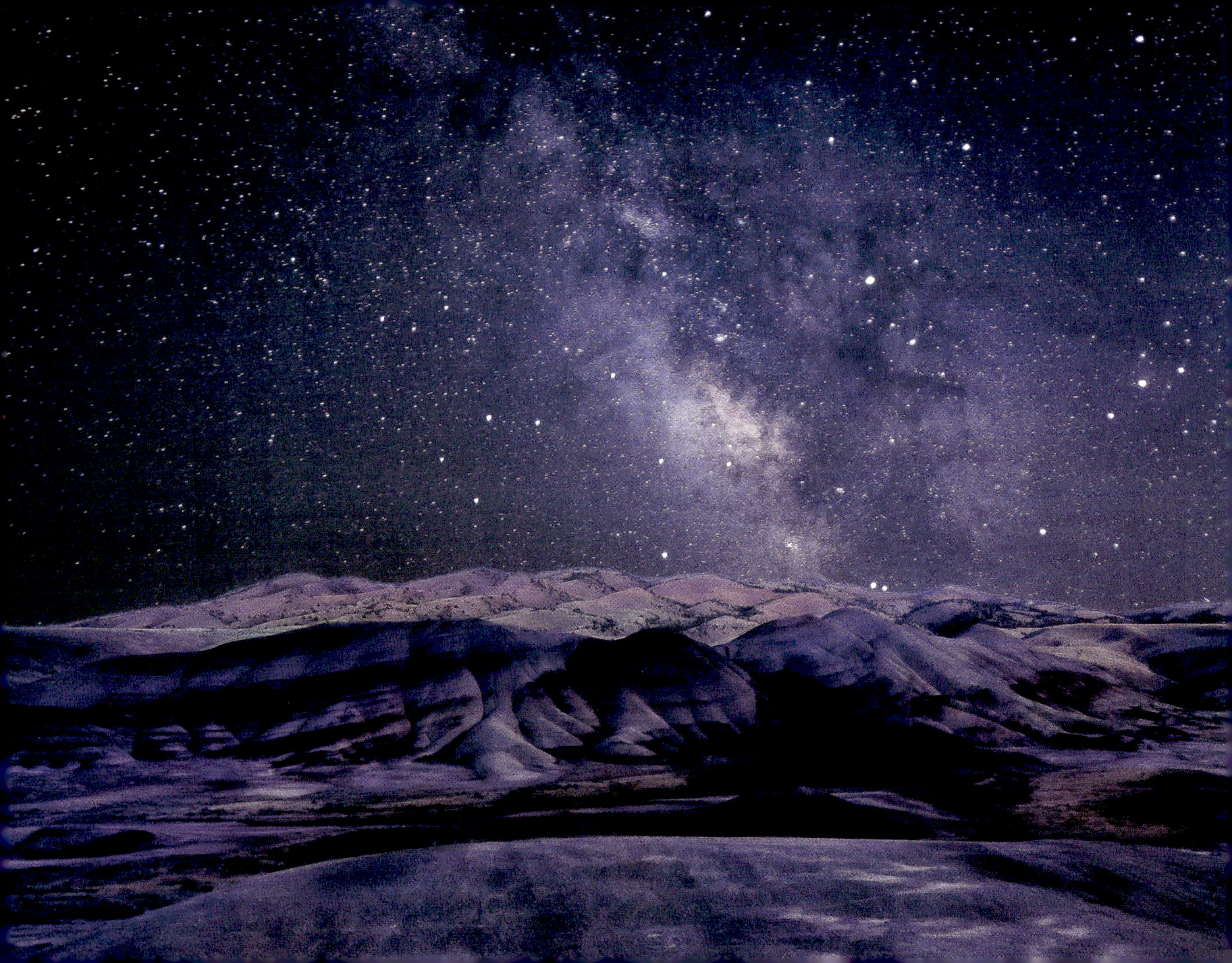

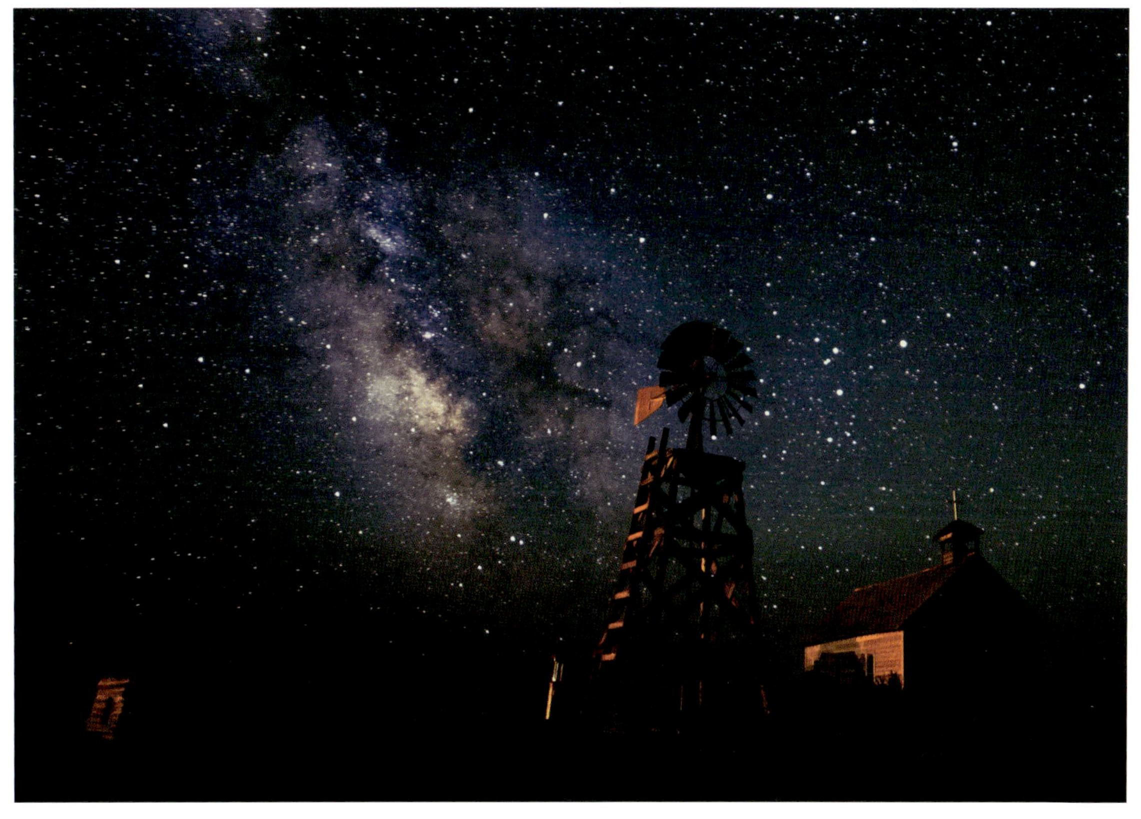

Milky Way over Painted Hills. *Photo by Clem Paslack*

Milky Way over Fort Rock Museum. *Photo by Clem Paslack*

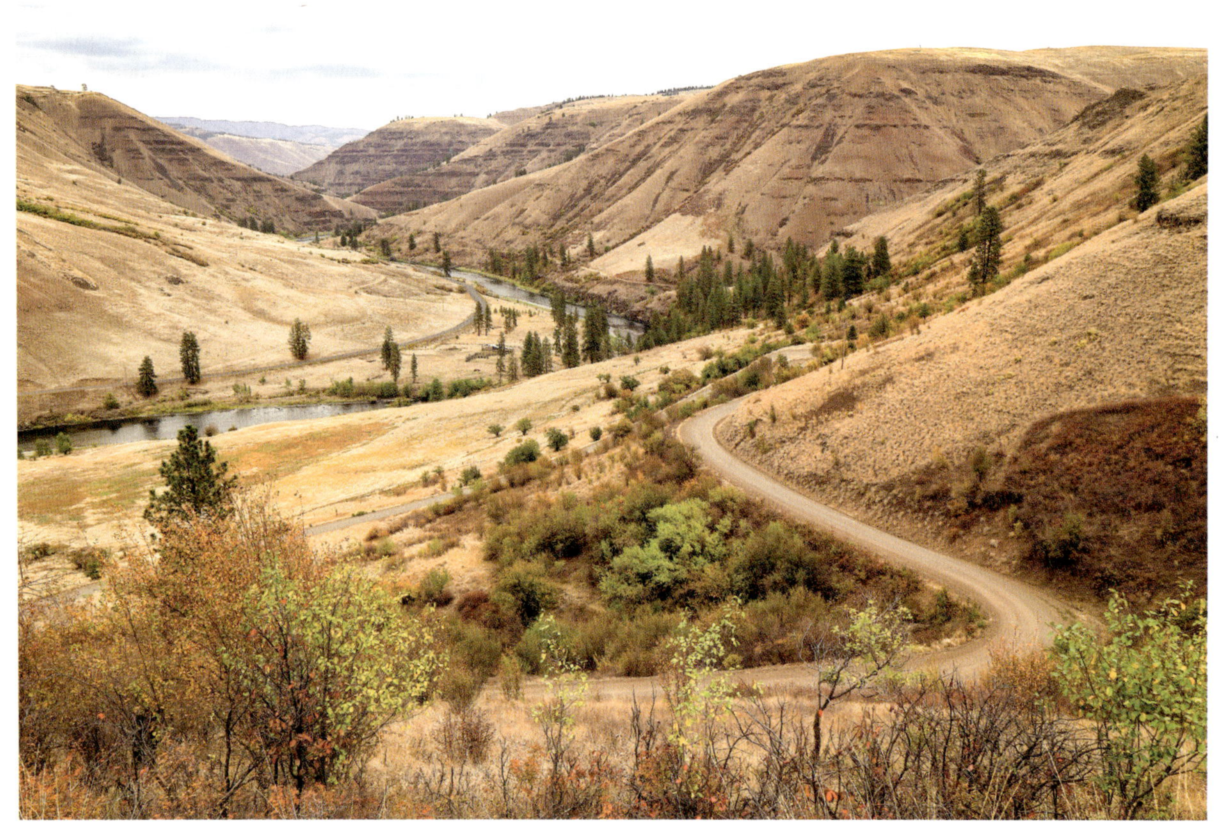

Grande Ronde Canyon, near Troy. *Photo by Terry Fisher*

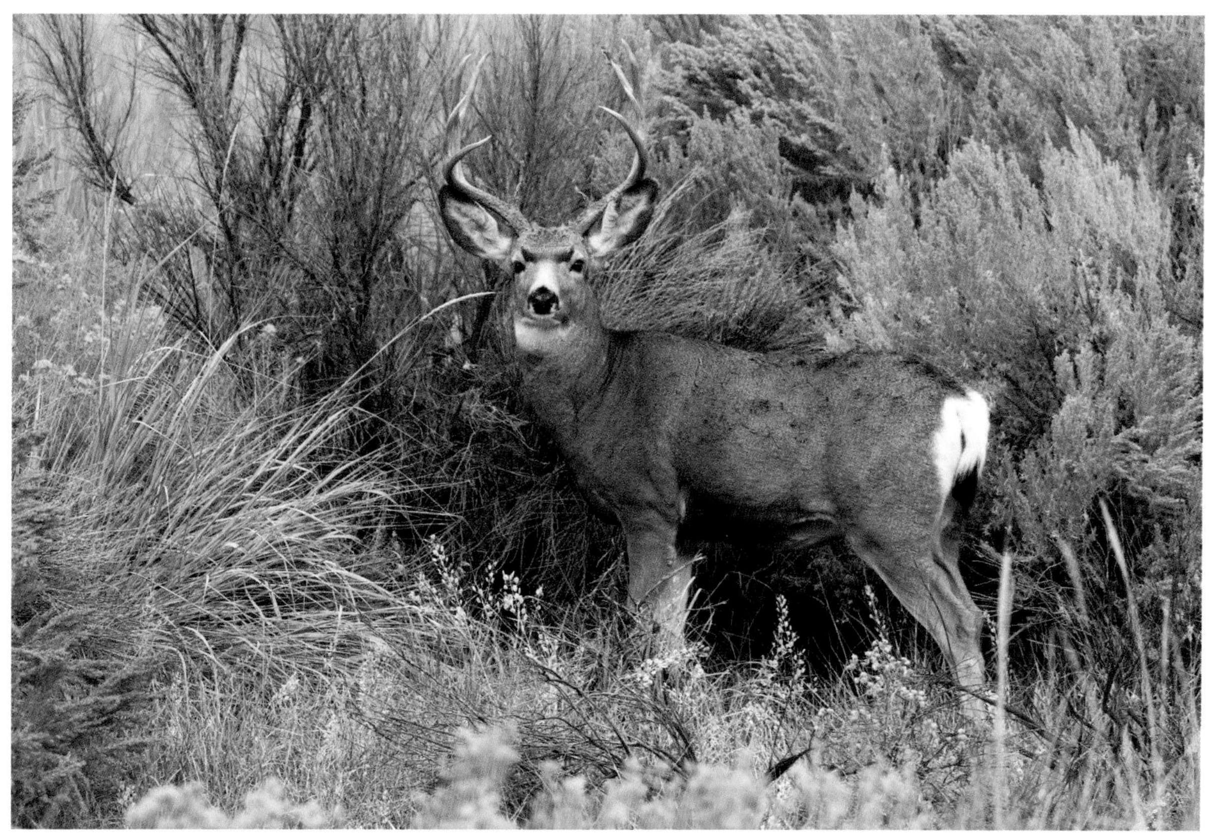

Mule deer buck in Malheur National Wildlife Refuge.
Photo by Dan Elster

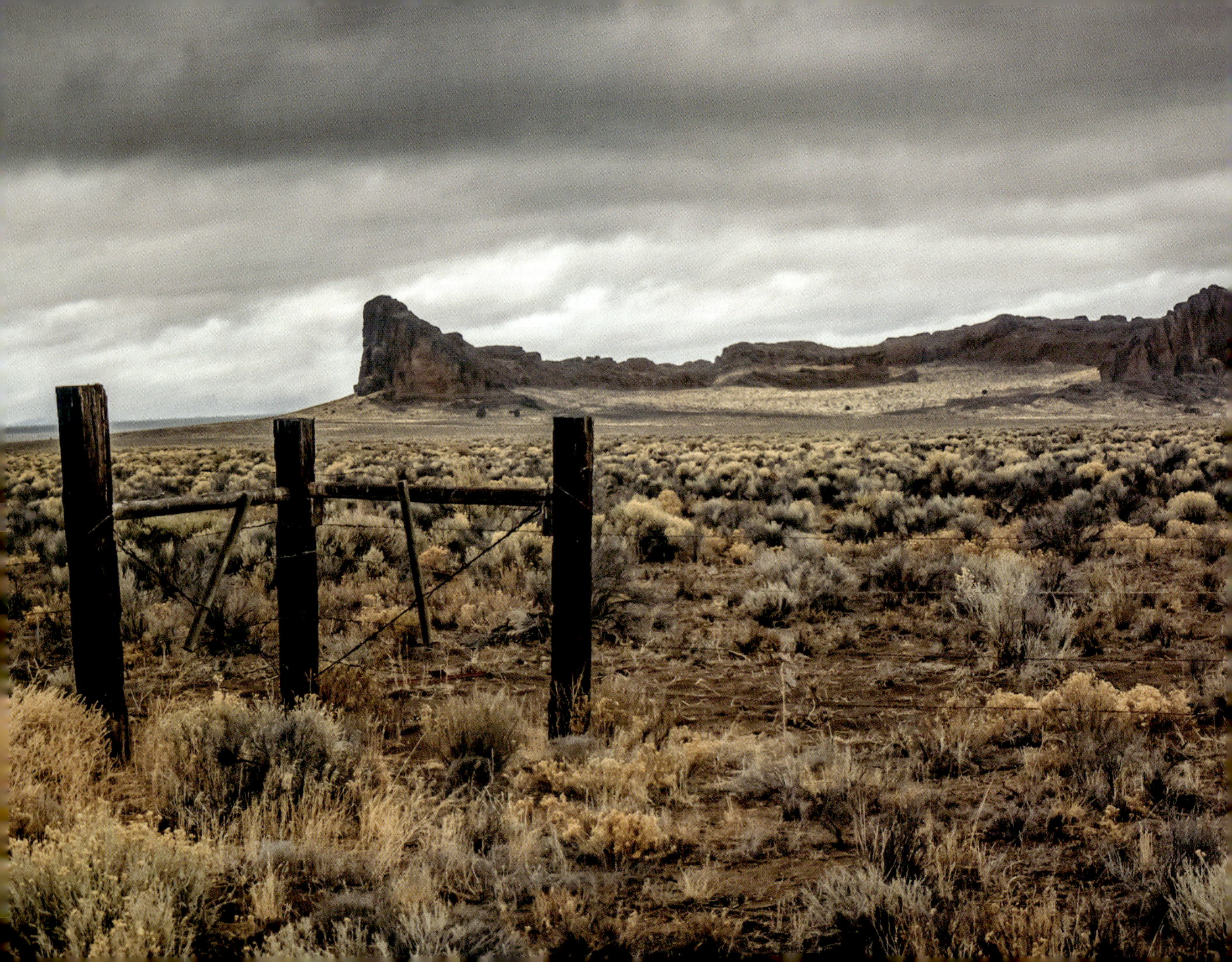

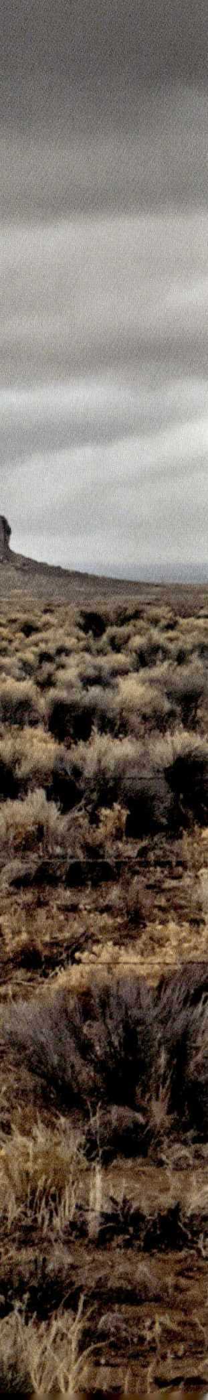

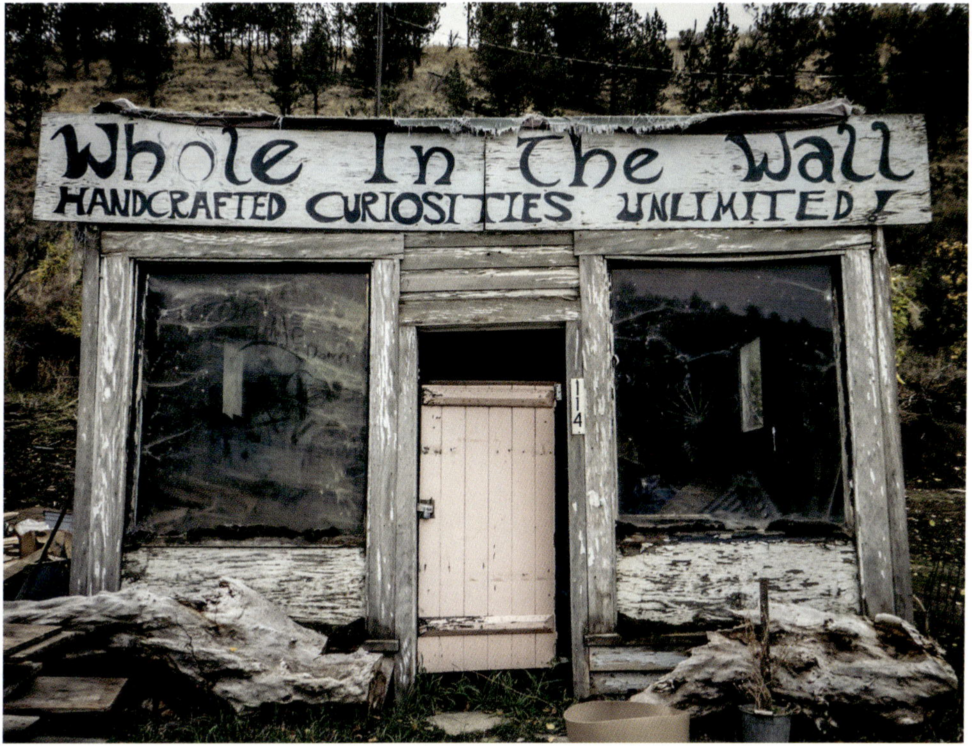

Fort Rock State Natural Area. The landmark, resembling a fort, sits on a volcanic ice-age lakebed. *Photo by Randy Bryan*

Abandoned store, Mitchell. *Photo by Diana Standing*

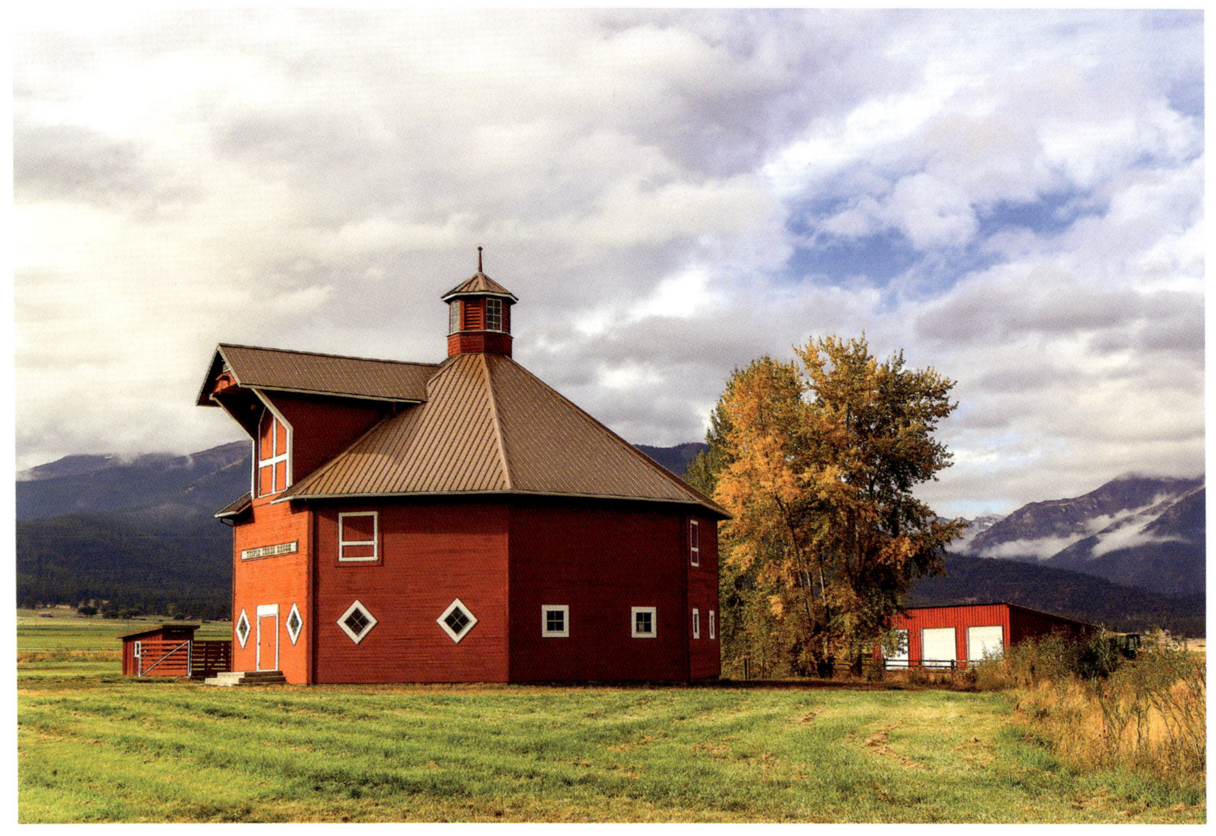

Red round barn at Triple Creek Ranch, near Joseph.
Photo by Terry Fisher

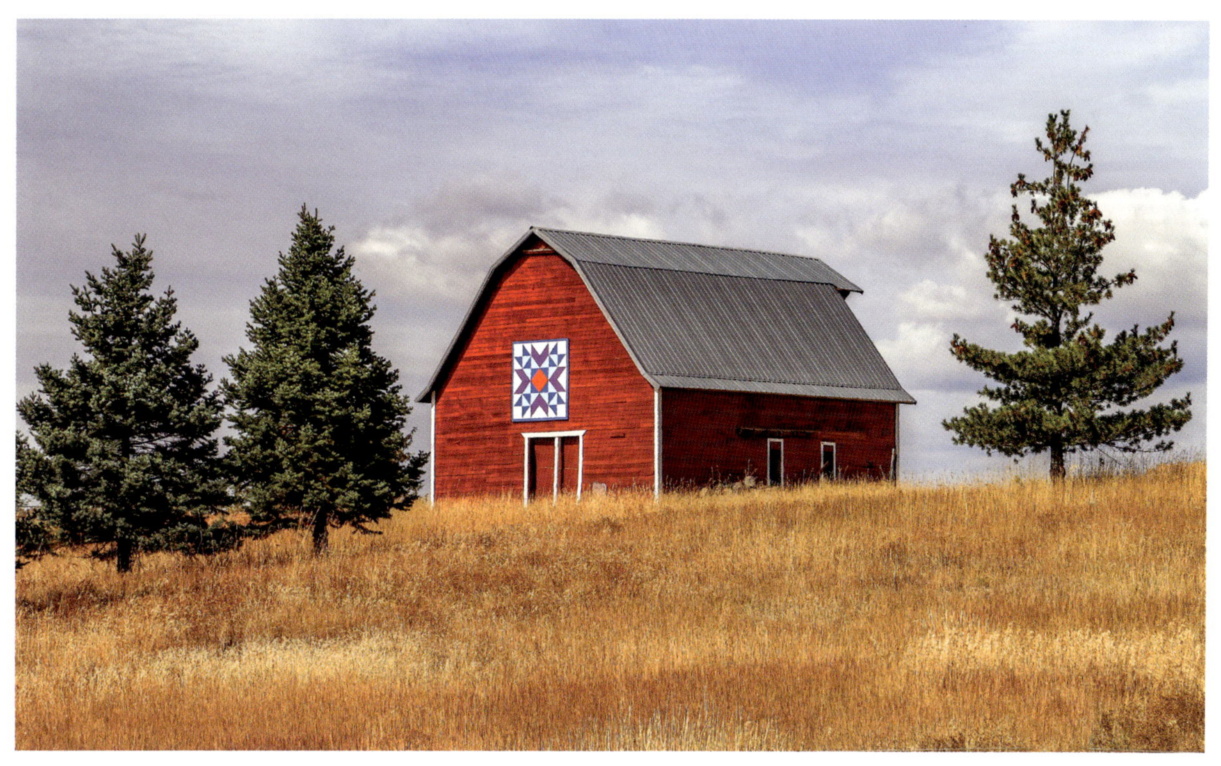

The American Quilt Trail began as a grassroots effort in 2001. More than 7,000 quilt blocks have now been added to barns across the United States, like this one in Flora. *Photo by Terry Fisher*

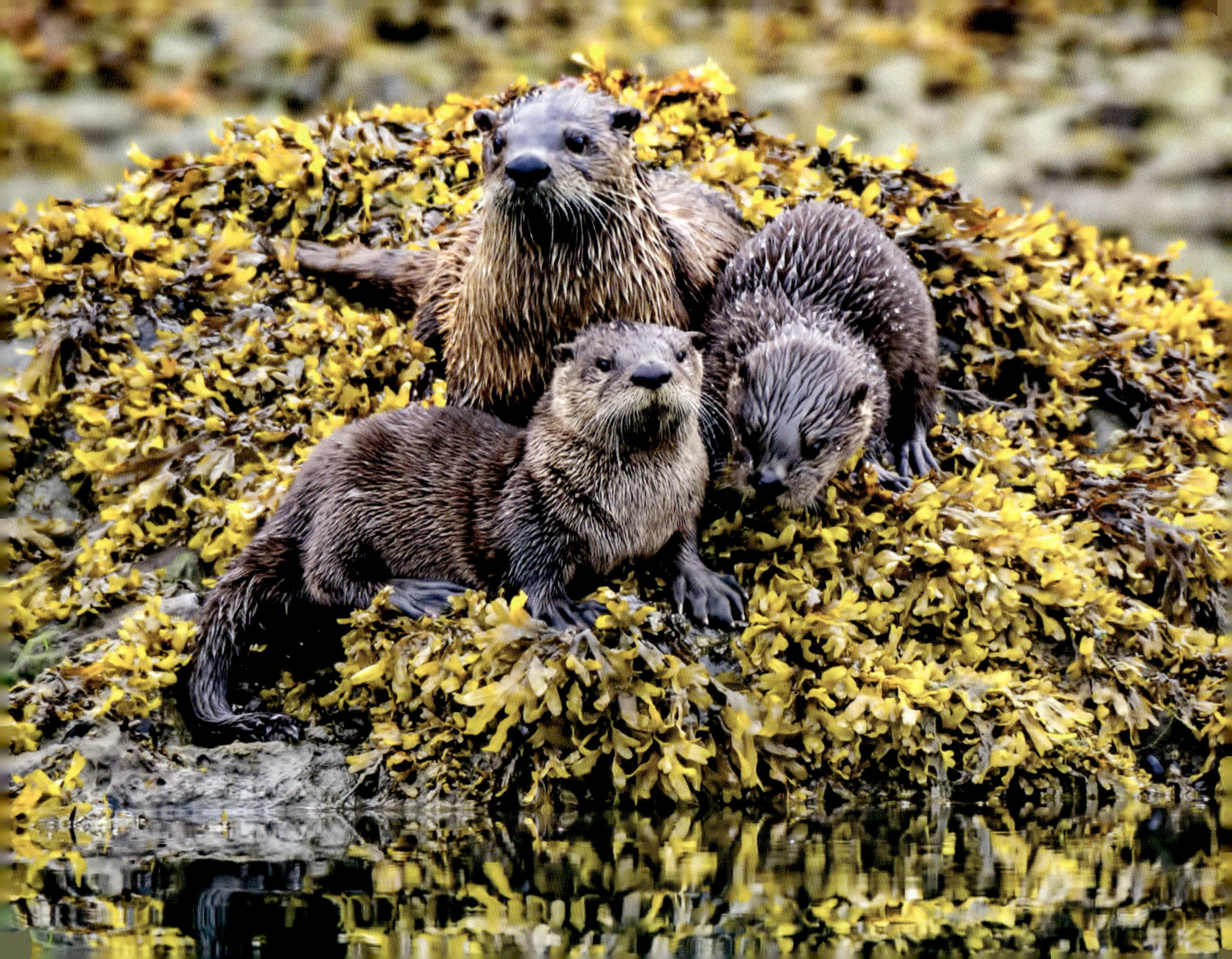

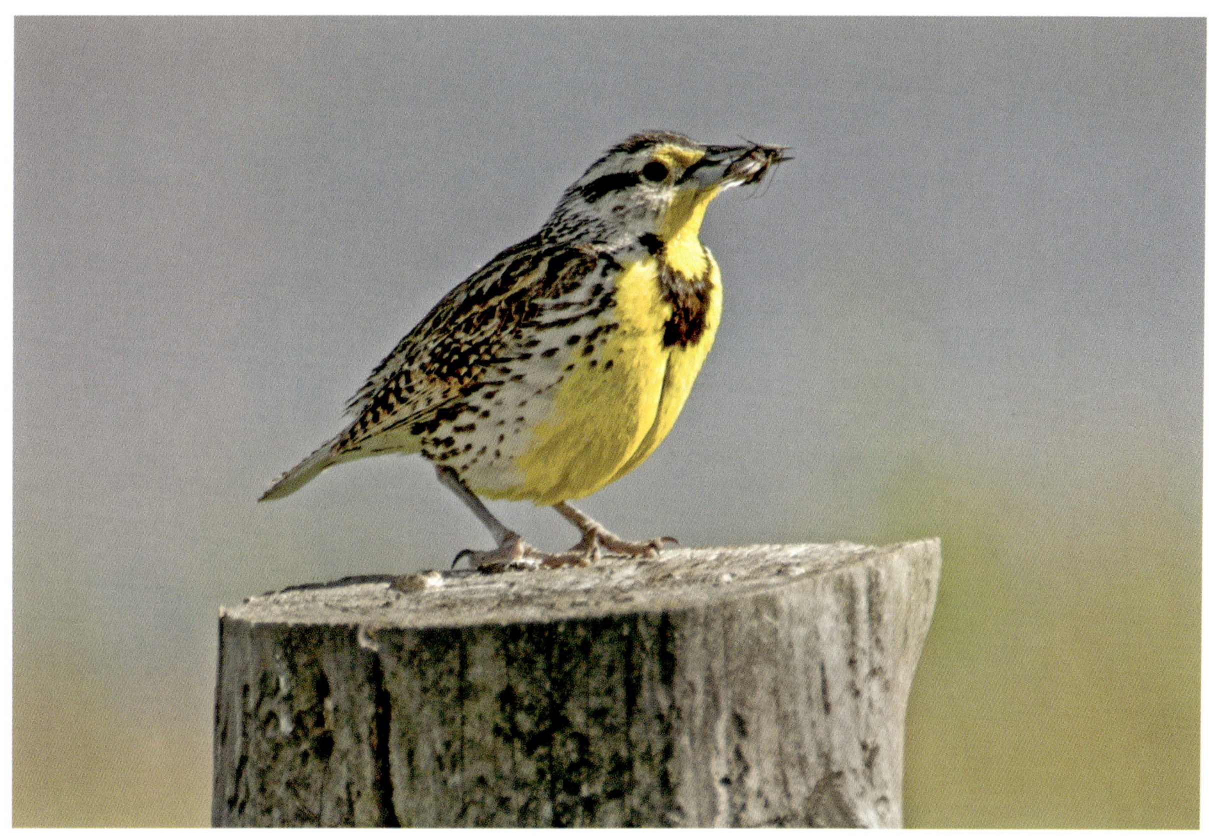

River otters. *Photo by Nick Viani*

Western meadowlark in Malheur National Wildlife Refuge. *Photo by George F. Peterson*

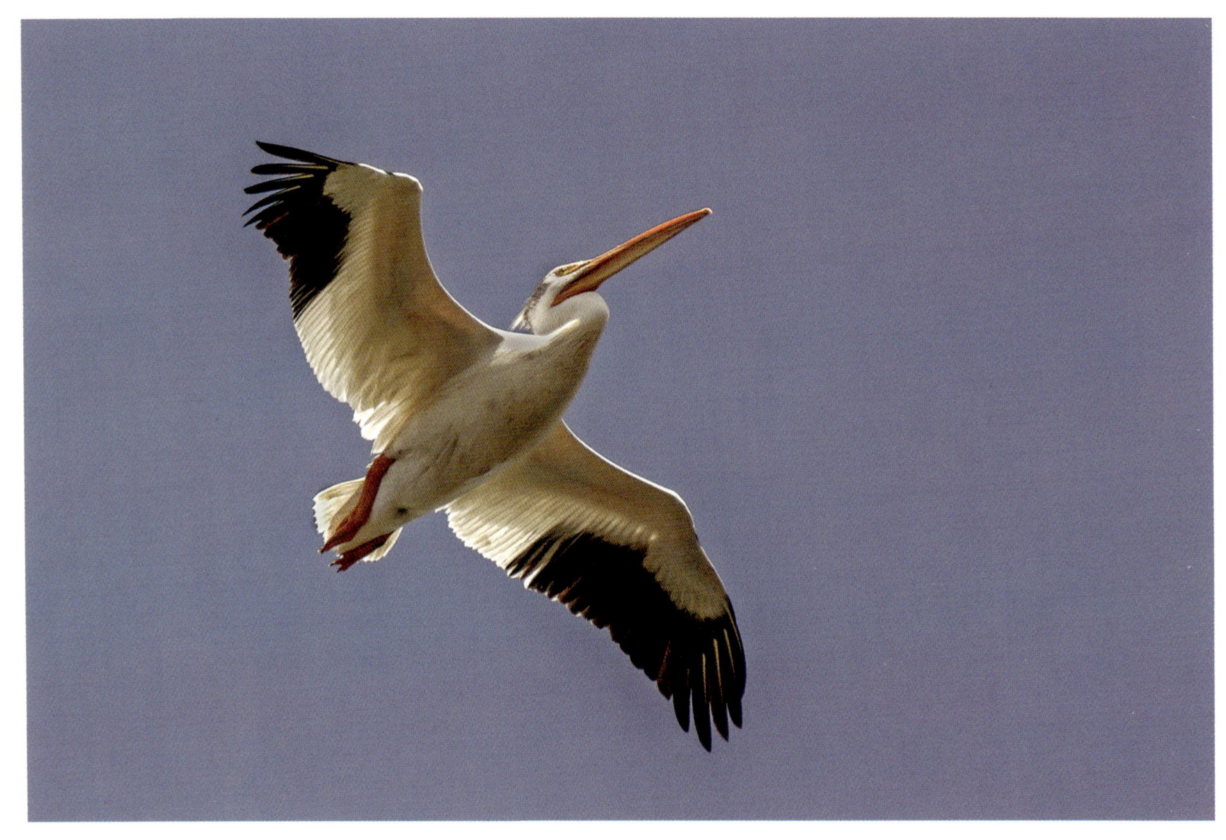

White pelican. *Photo by George F. Peterson*

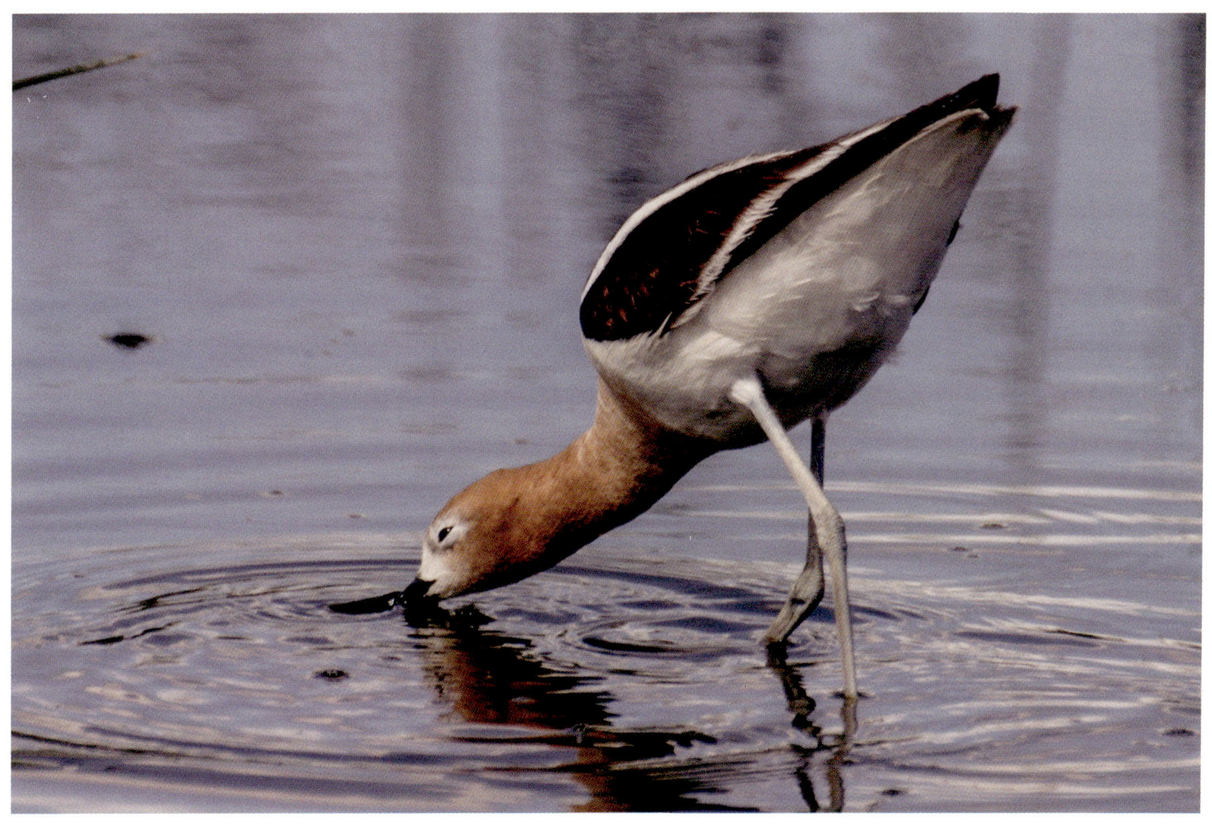

American avocet. *Photo by George F. Peterson*

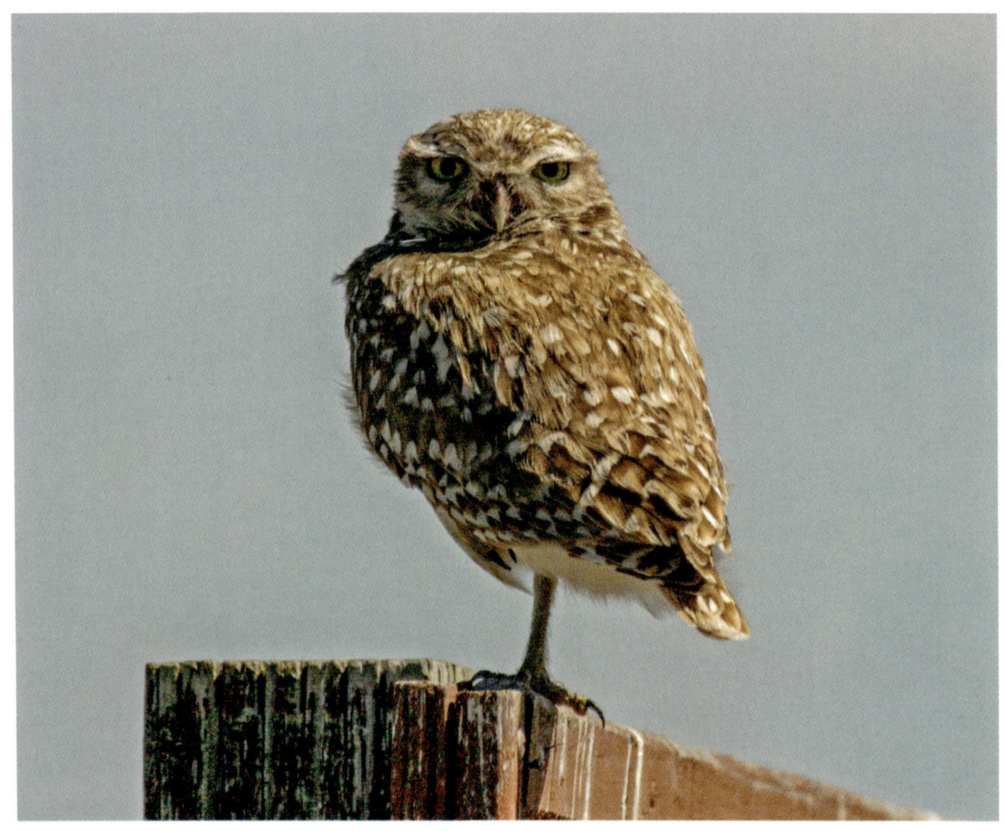

Burrowing owl in Malheur National Wildlife Refuge.
Photo by George F. Peterson

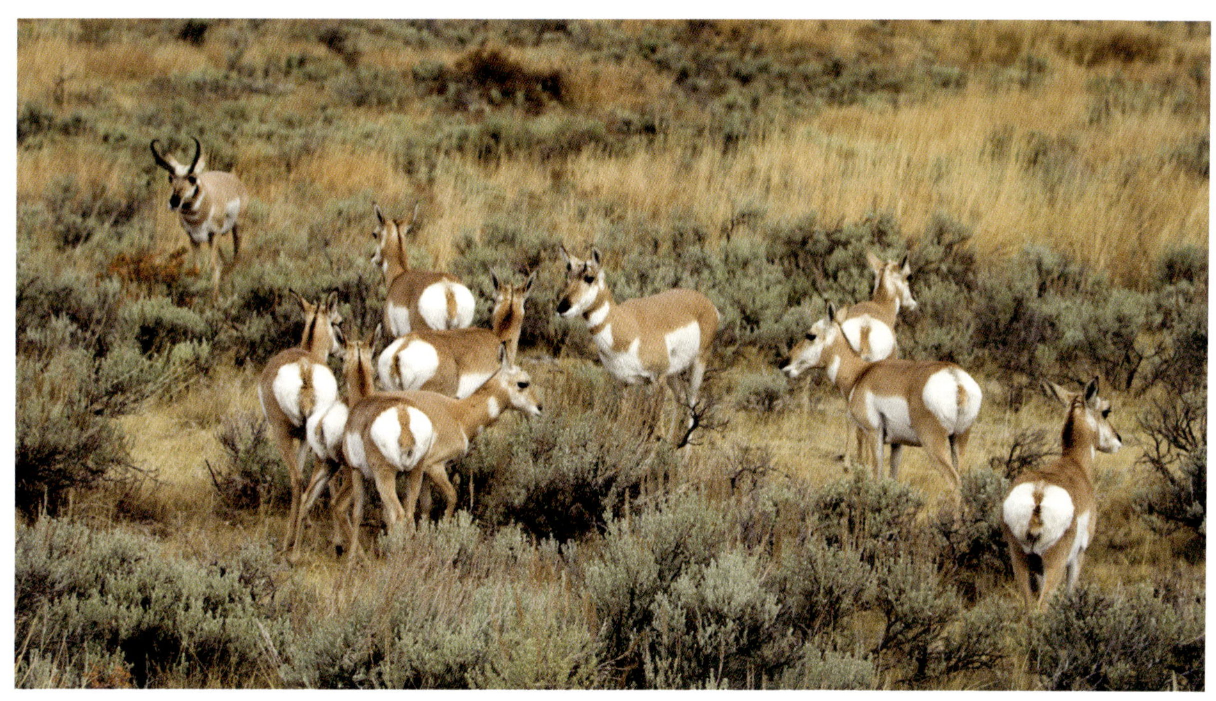

Pronghorn harem. *Photo by Howard Hunt*

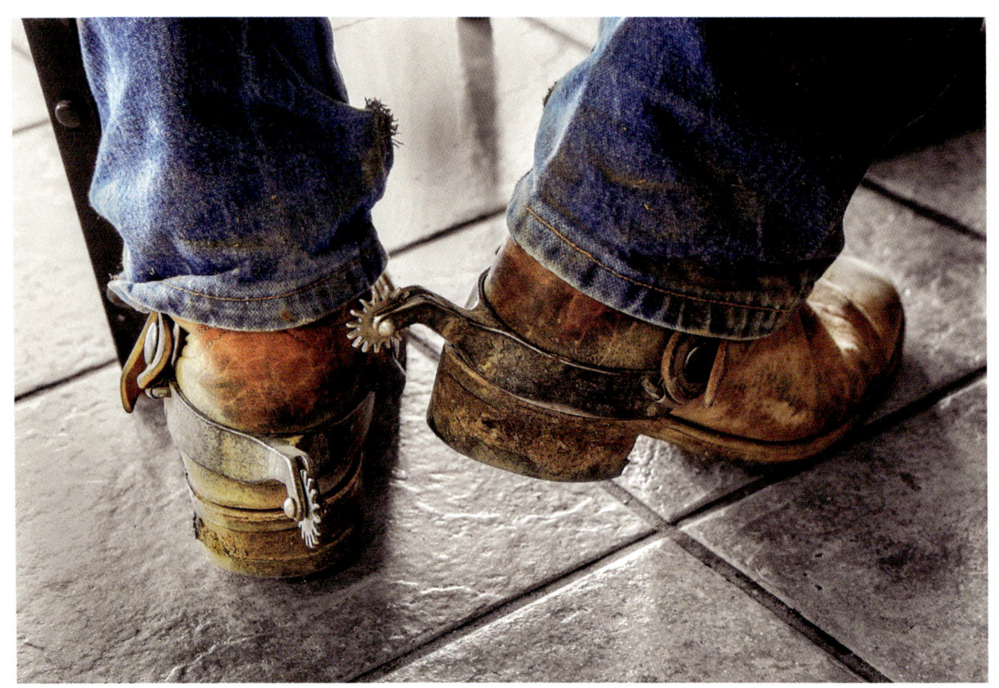

Cowboy boots. *Photo by Neal R. Thompson*

Cattle rancher near Malheur National Wildlife Refuge. *Photo by George F. Peterson*

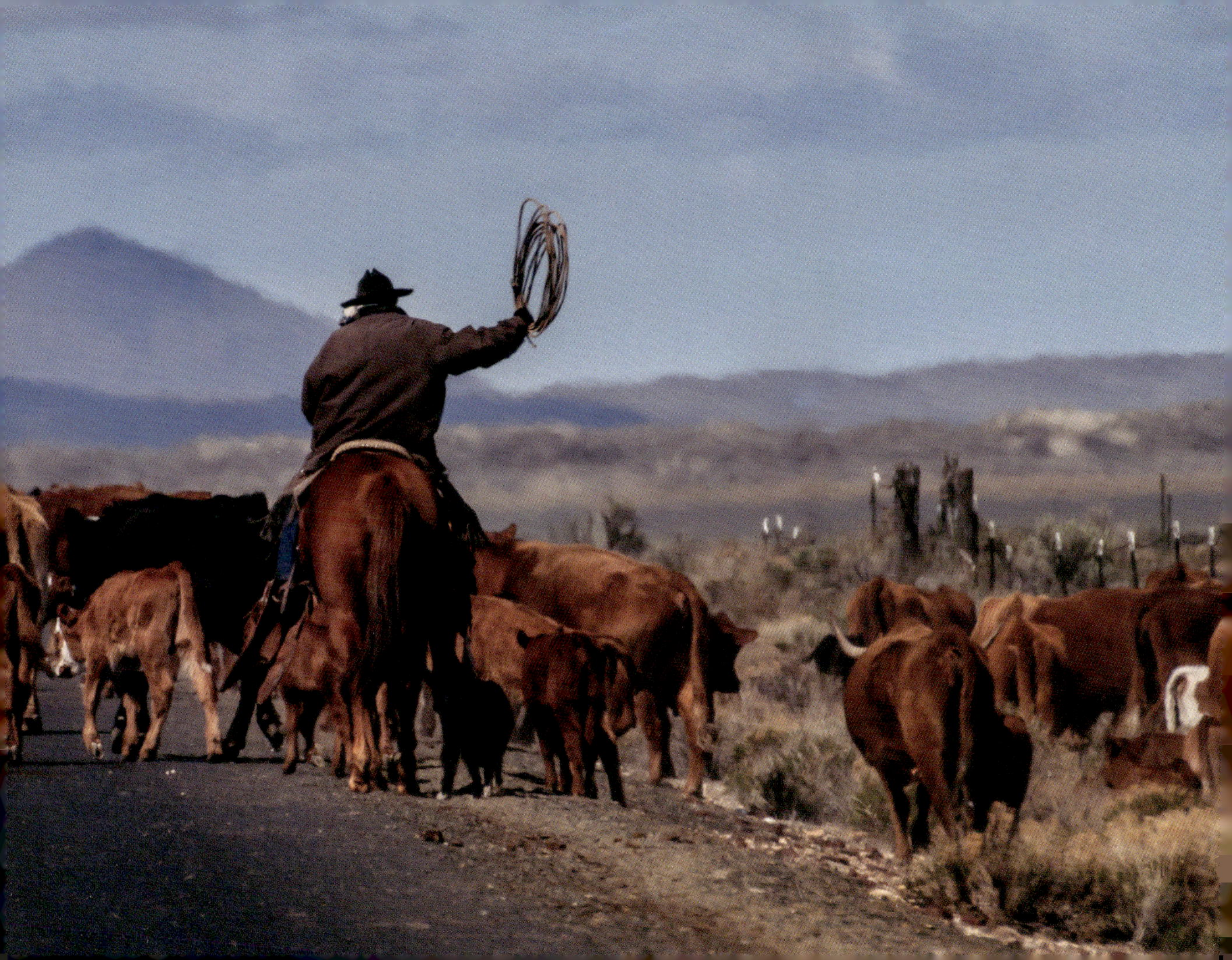

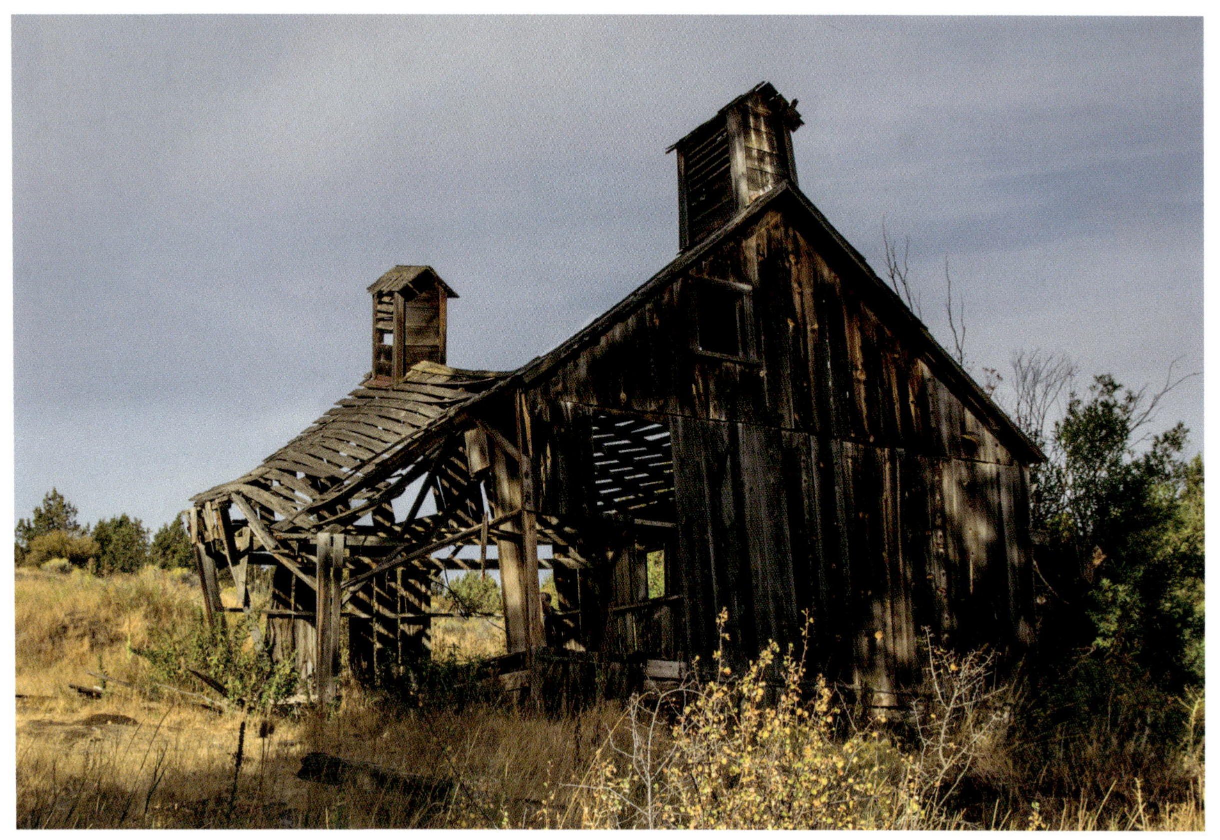

Abandoned building in ghost town of Shaniko.
Photo by George F. Peterson

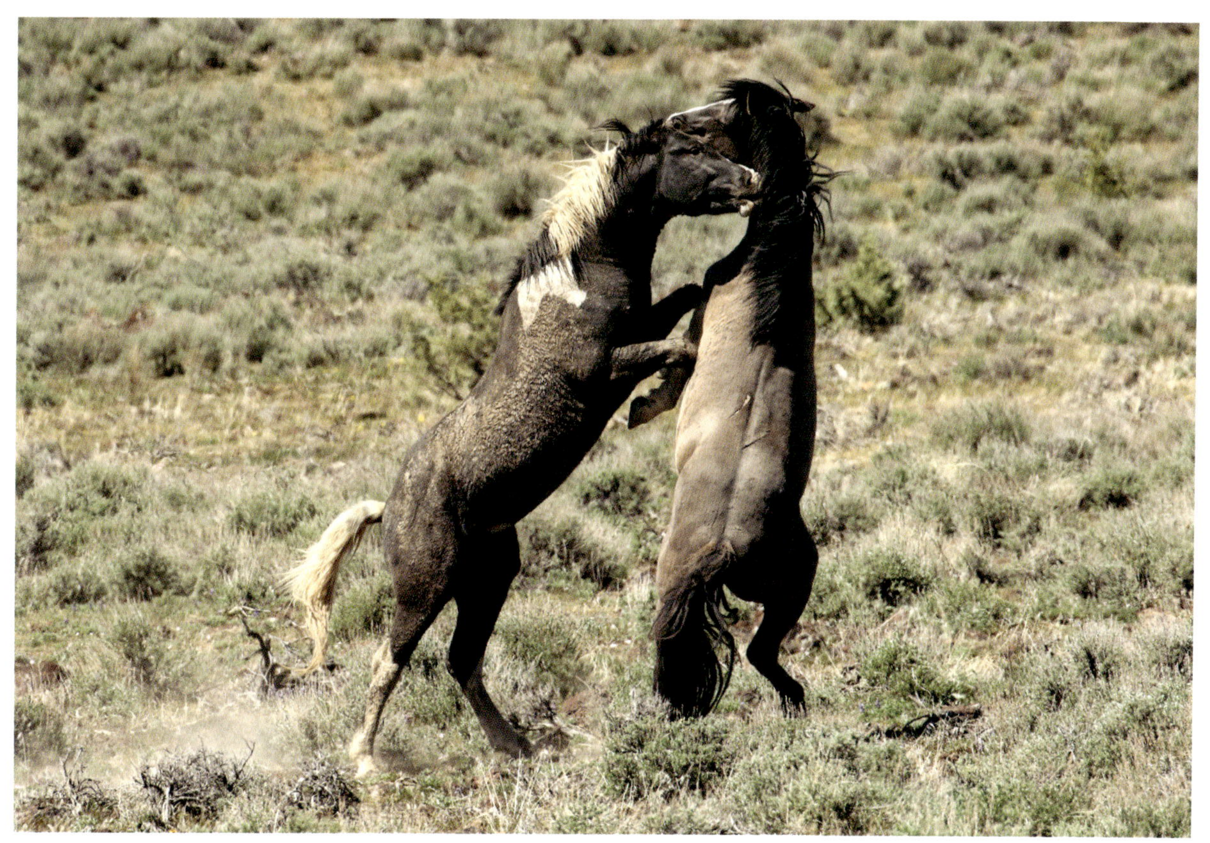

Wild mustangs, Steens Mountain. *Photo by Dan Elster*

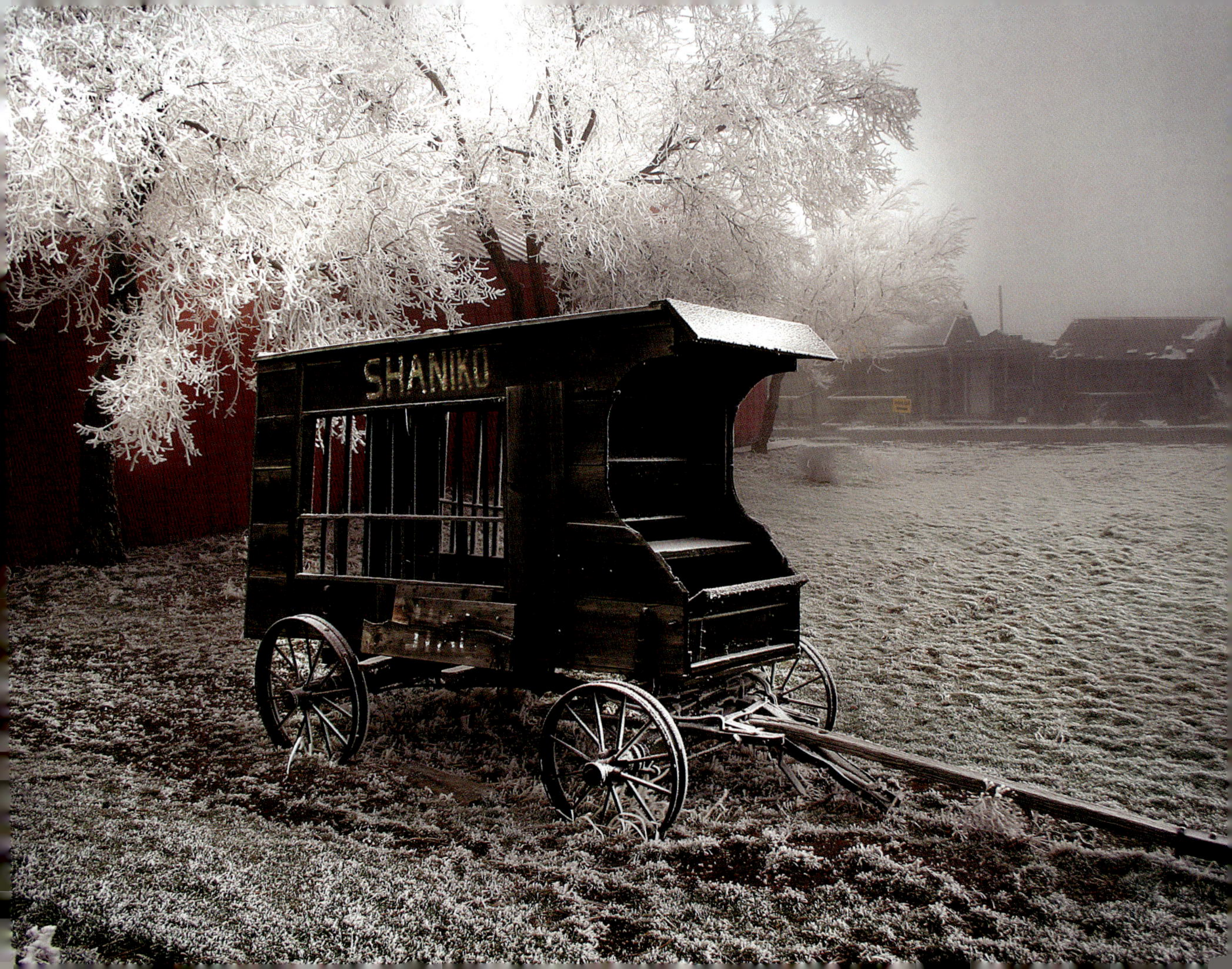
SHANIKO

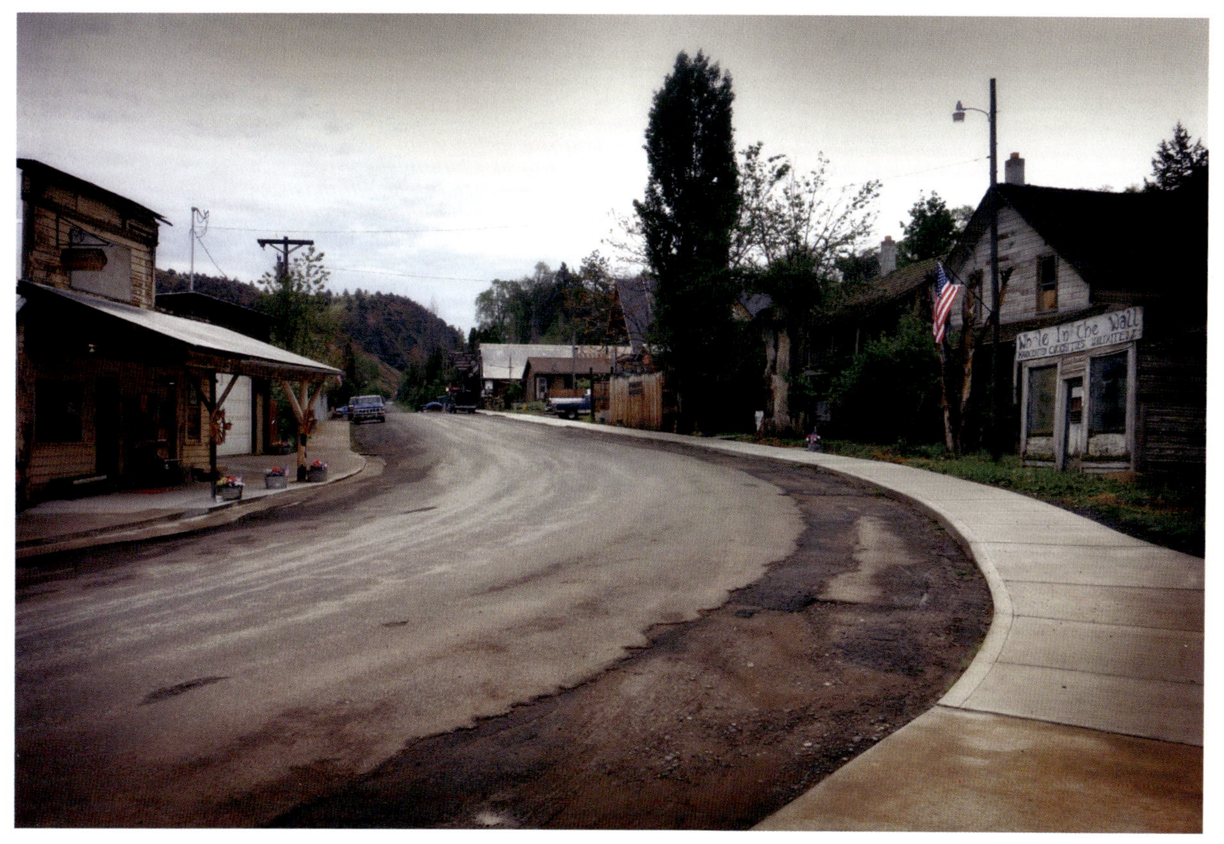

Stagecoach in Shaniko. *Photo by Neal R. Thompson*

Town of Mitchell, "Gateway to the Painted Hills," established 1873, population 130. *Photo by John Kirk*

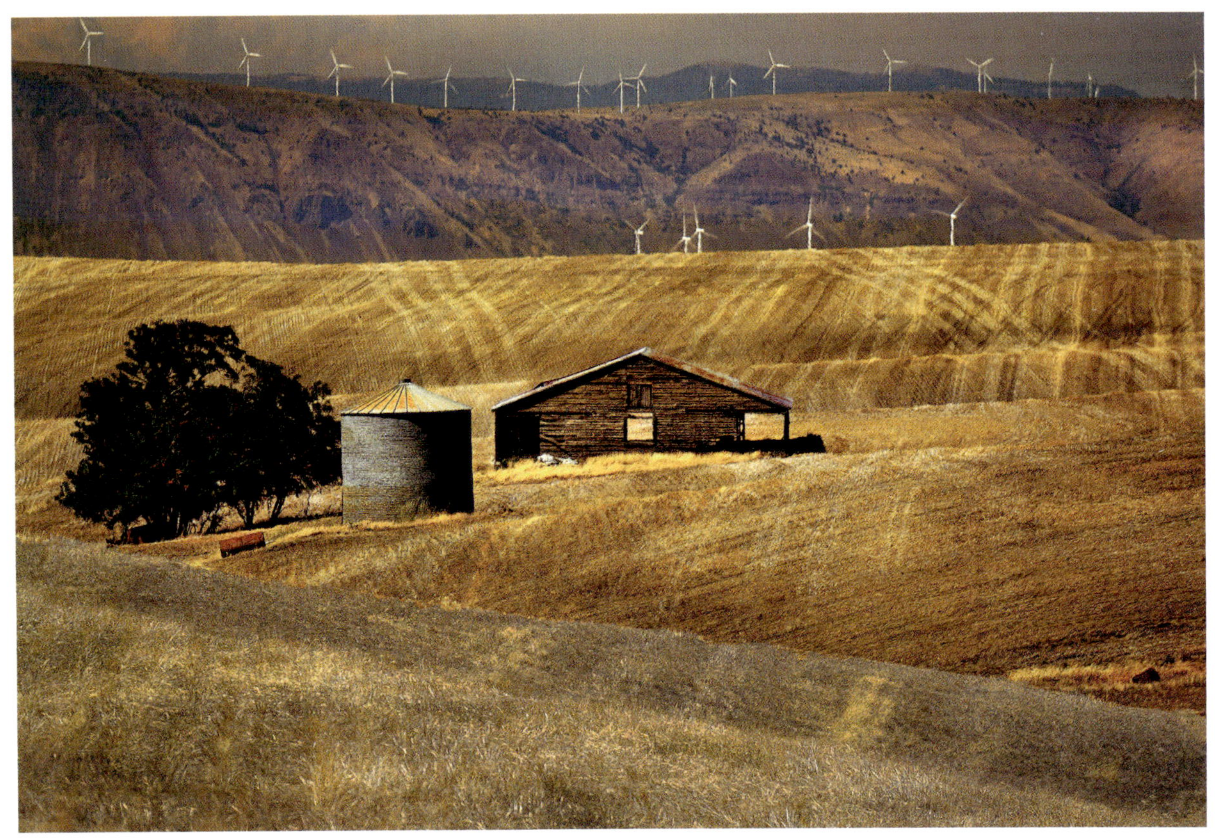

Wheat fields in Wasco. *Photo by Neal R. Thompson*

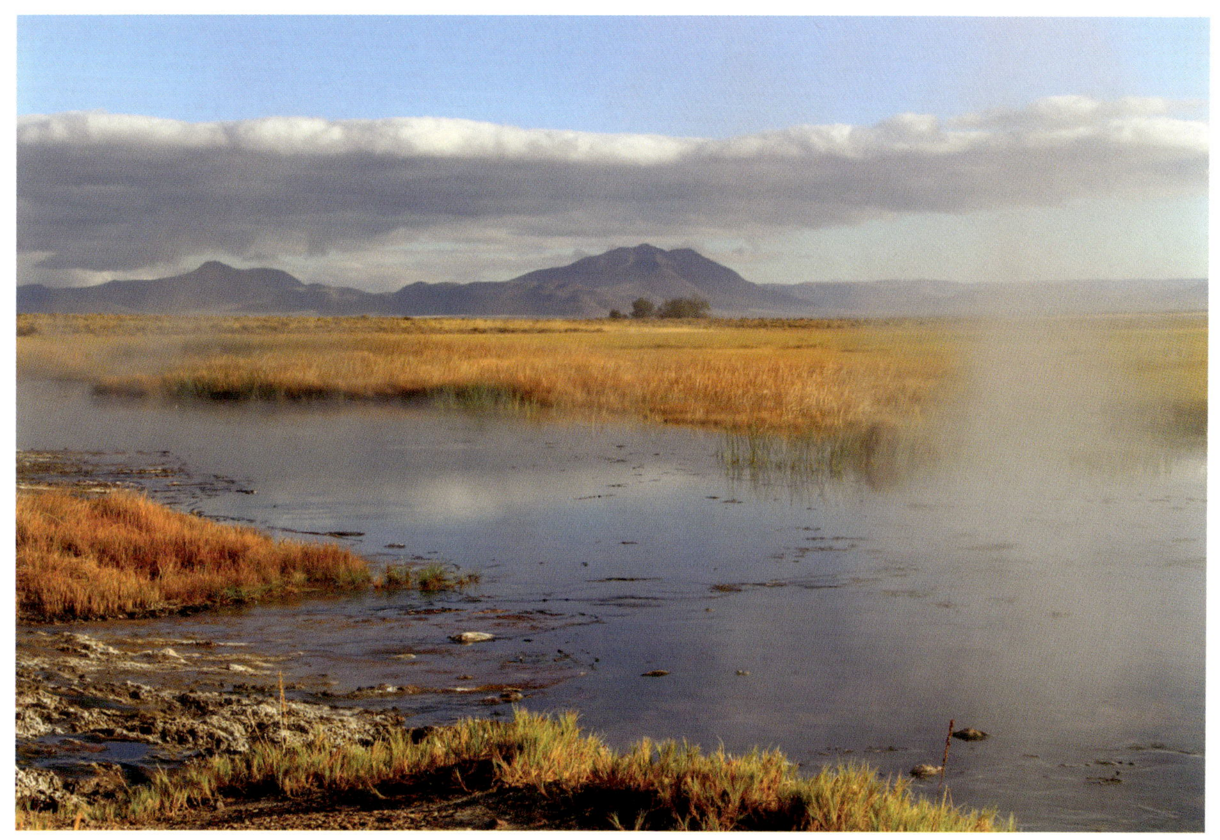

Alvord Hot Springs. *Photo by Diana Standing*

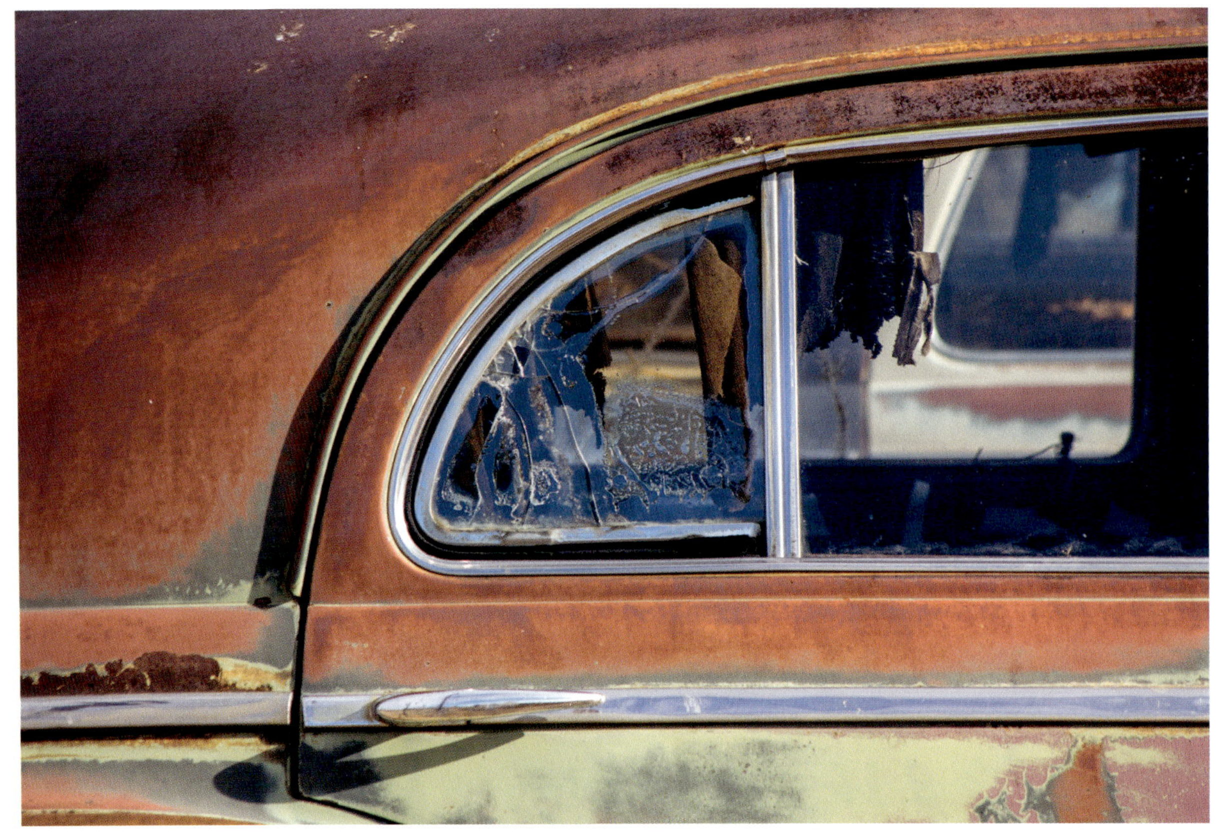

Rusted car, Shaniko. *Photo by George F. Peterson*

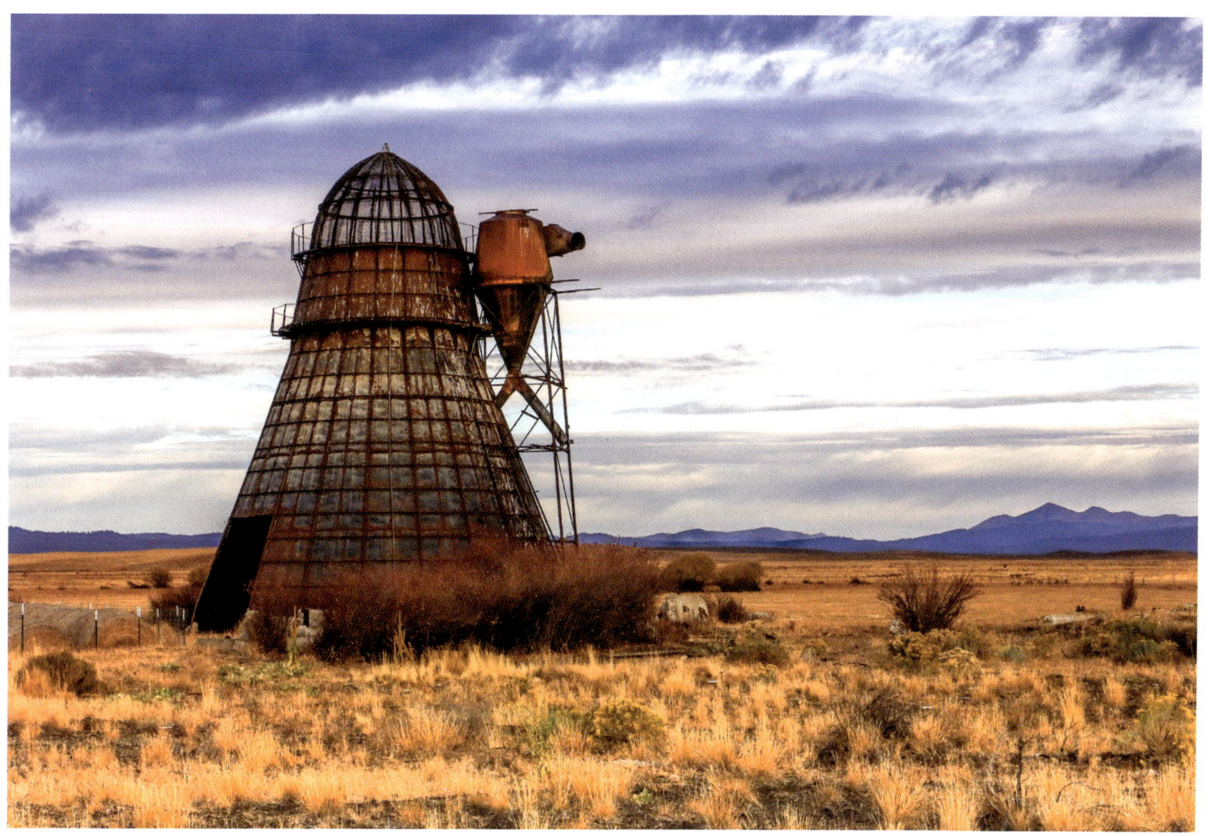

Wigwam burner near Seneca. Wood waste or sawdust burners like this were popular in logging yards and sawmills throughout Oregon until the 1970s. *Photo by Terry Fisher*

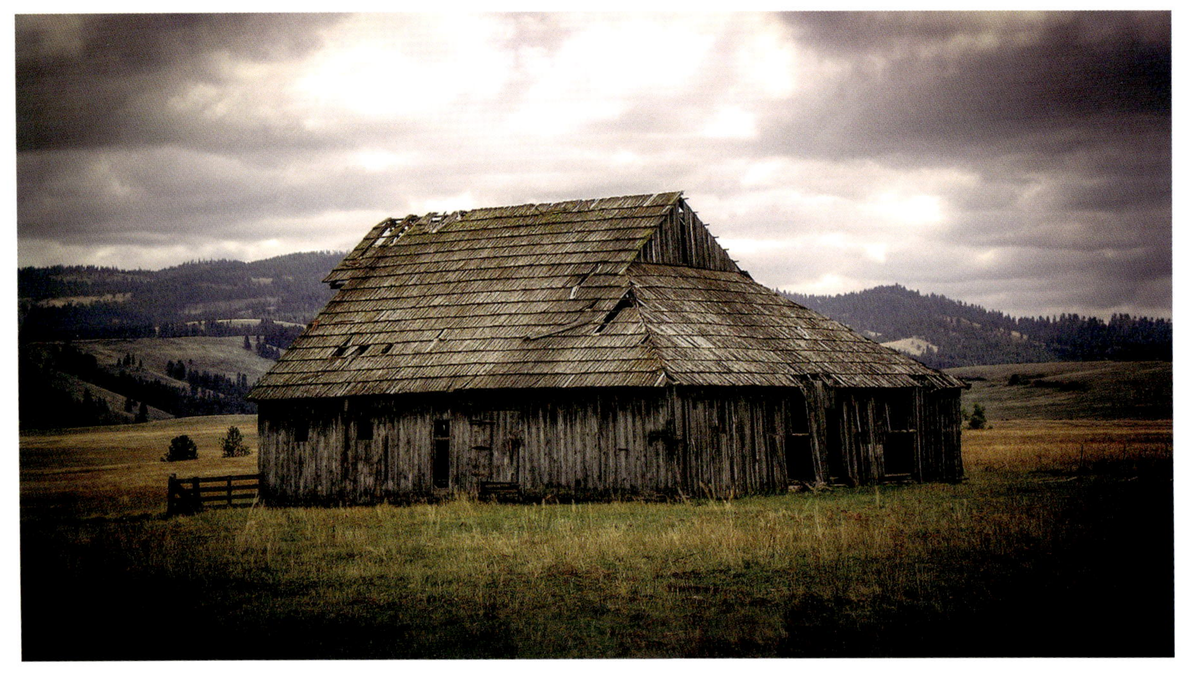

Barn in LaGrande. *Photo by Andrea Shapiro*

The town of Mitchell was built as a stage stop in the 1860s on the Dalles–John Day Military Road. *Photo by Diana Standing*

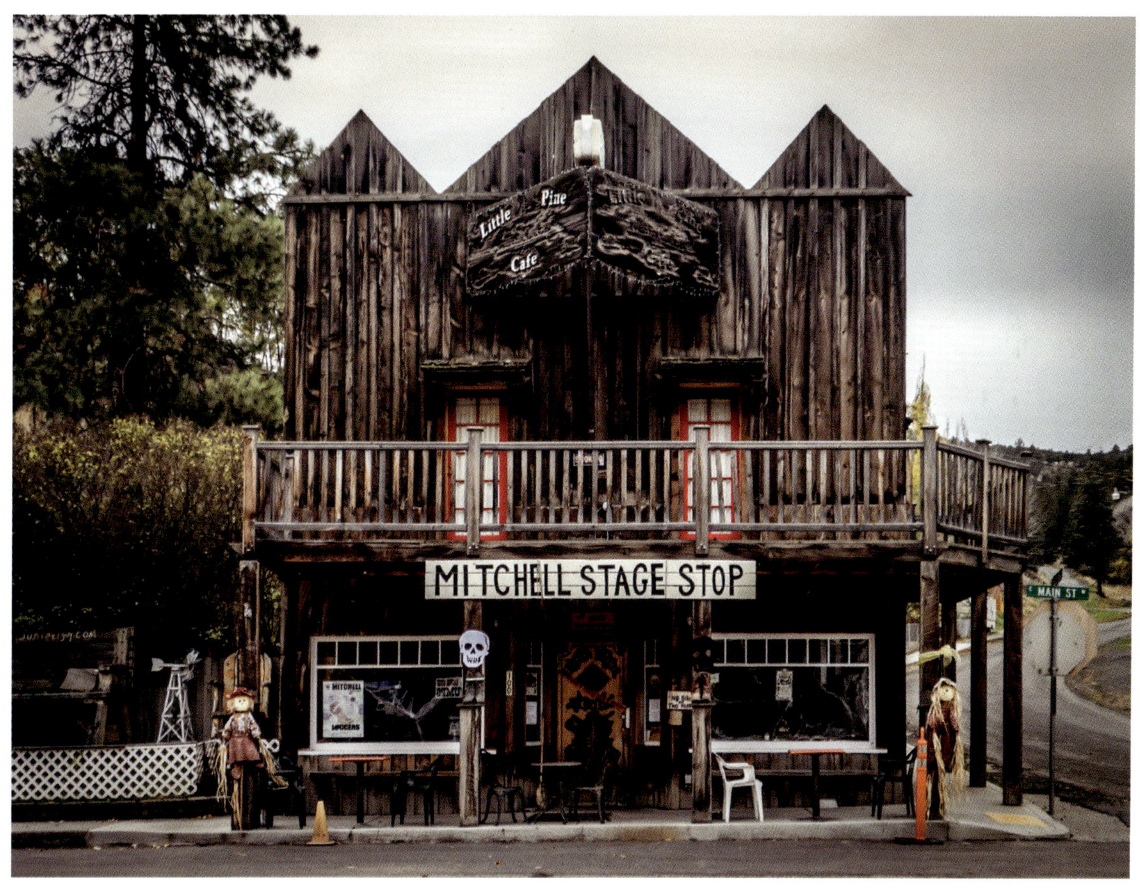
Little Pine Cafe
MITCHELL STAGE STOP
MAIN ST

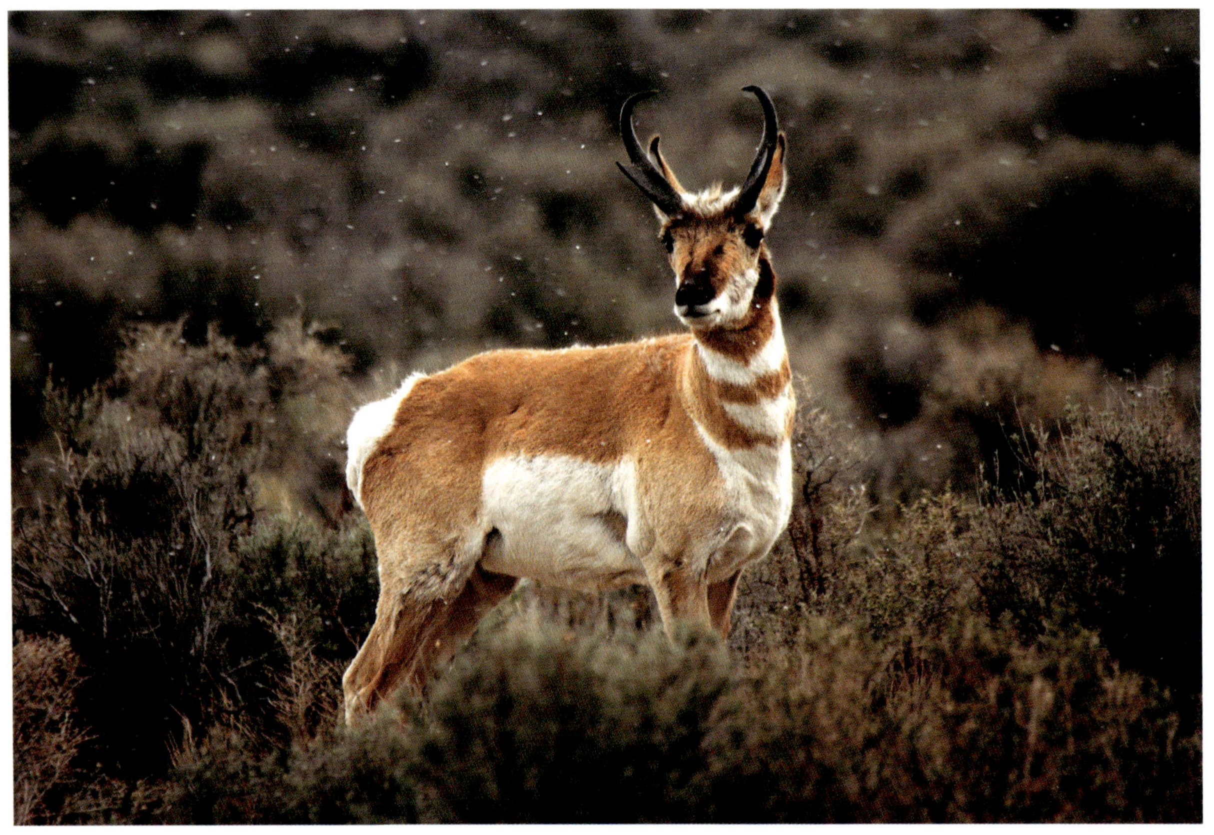

Pronghorn in the snow. *Photo by Dan Elster*

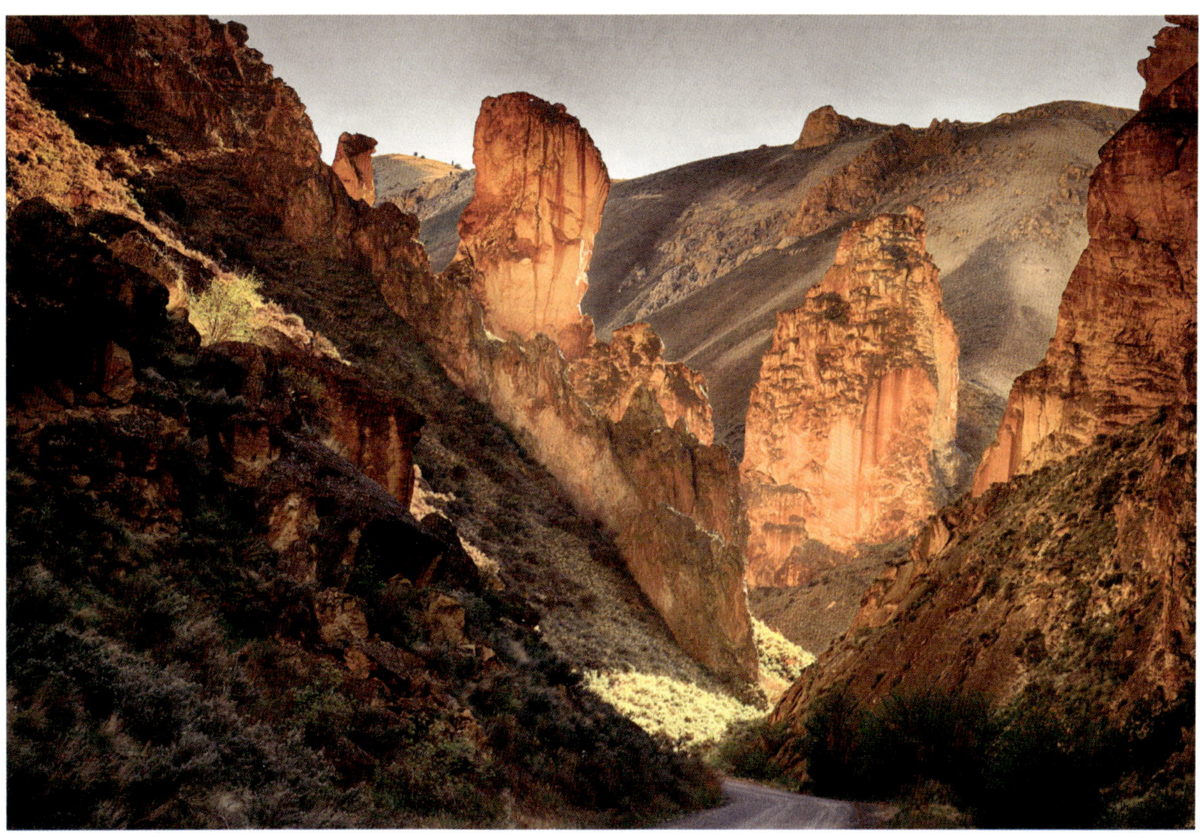

Leslie Gulch is a canyon in Malheur County with rock formations made of volcanic tuff. *Photo by John Kirk*

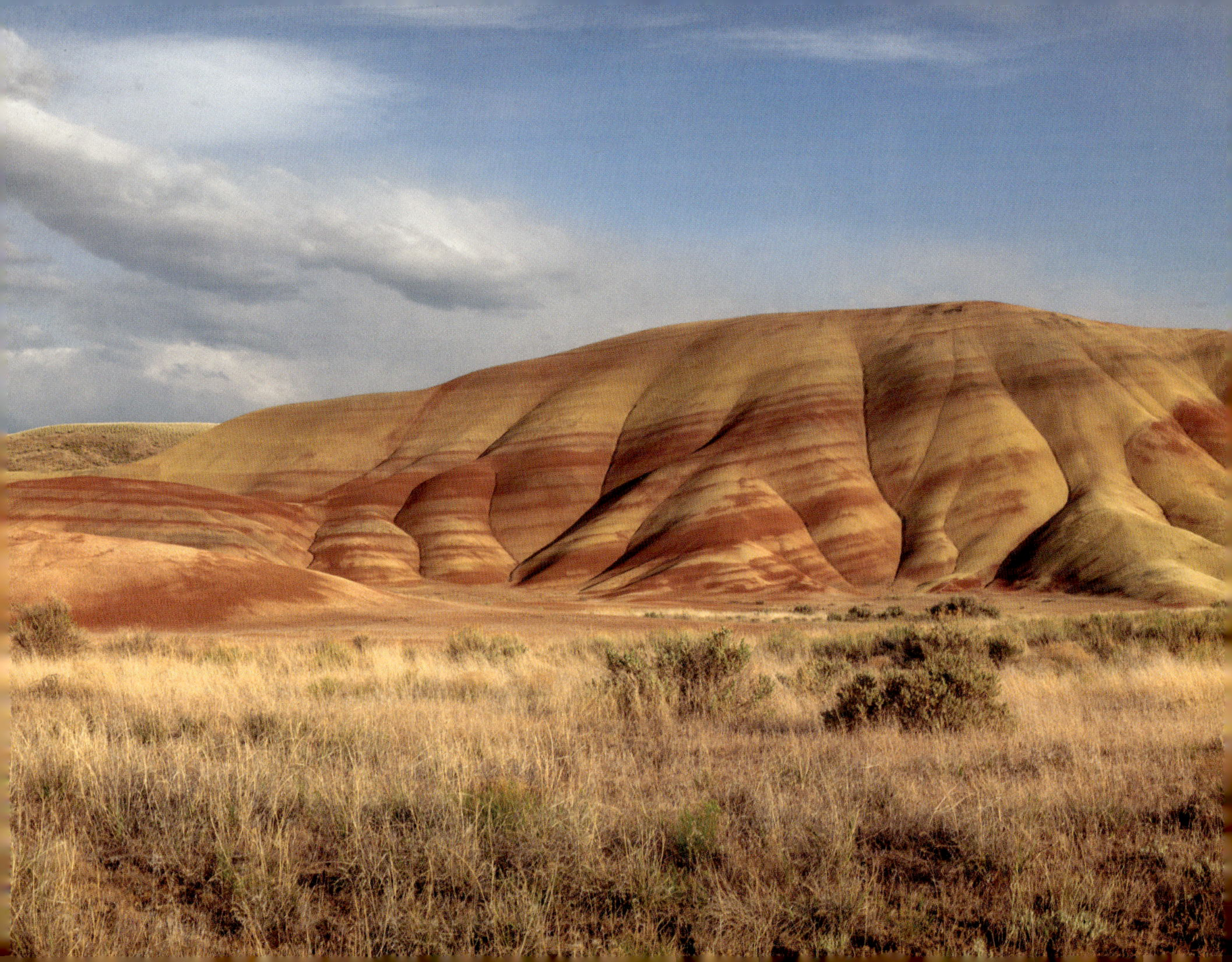

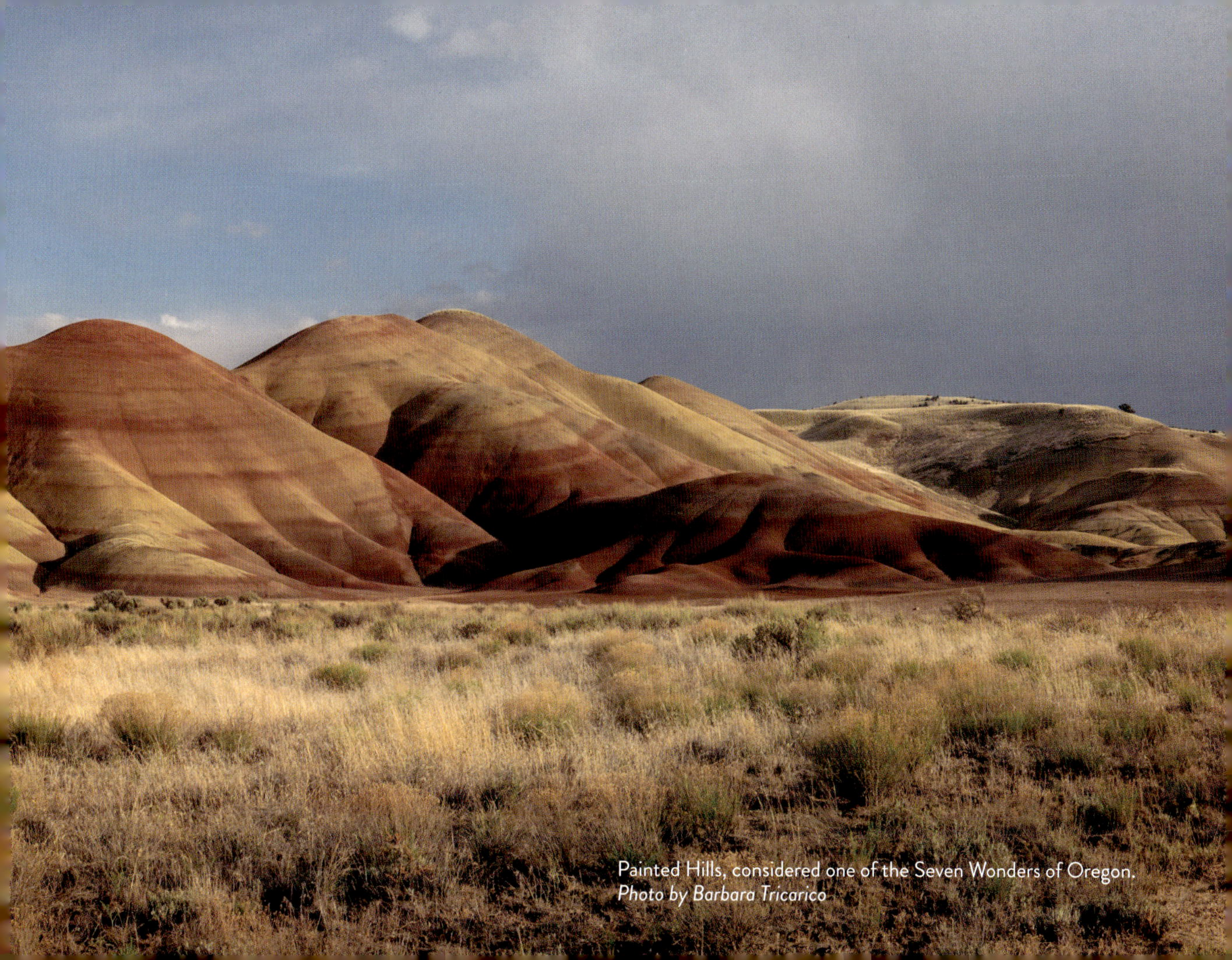

Painted Hills, considered one of the Seven Wonders of Oregon.
Photo by Barbara Tricarico

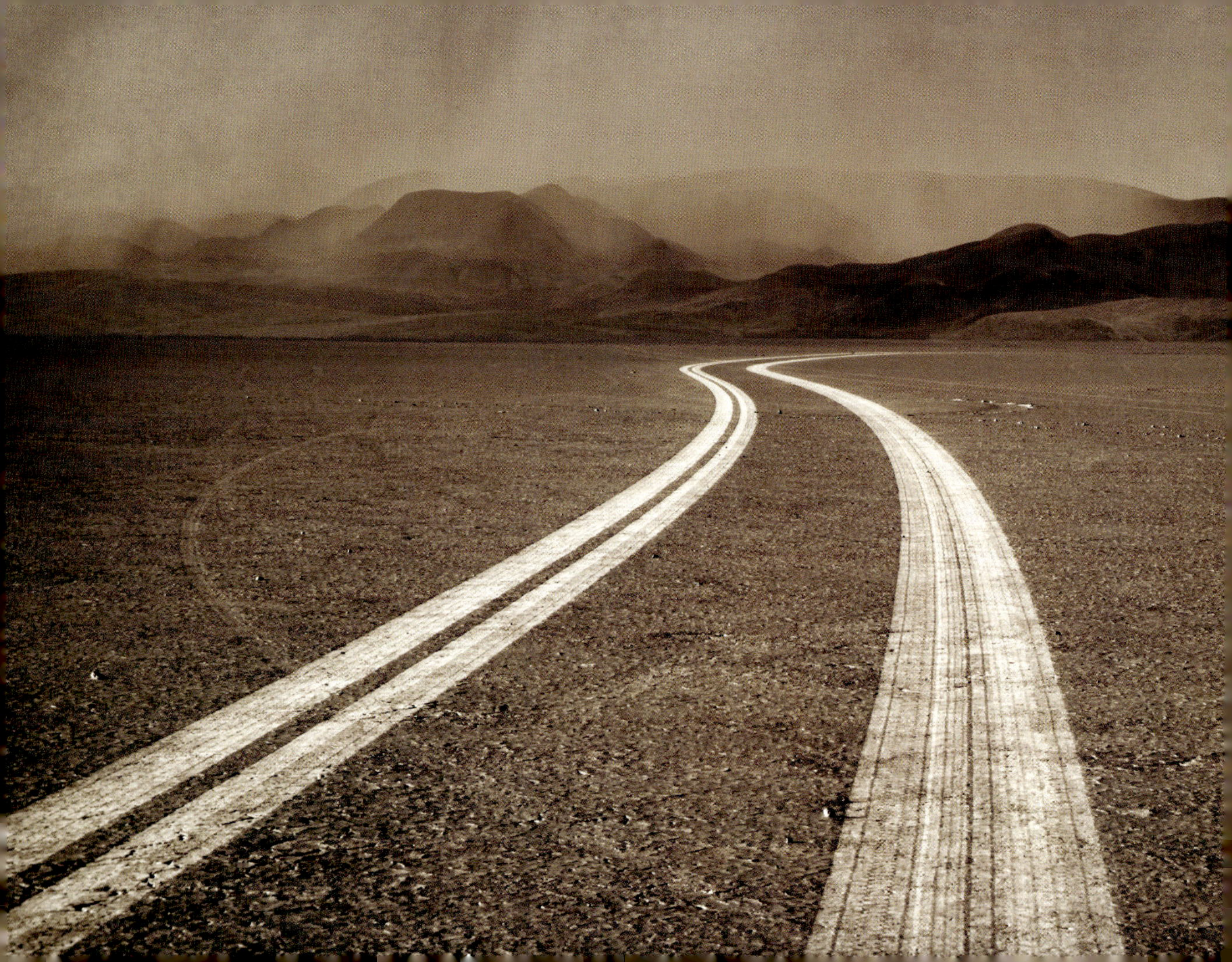

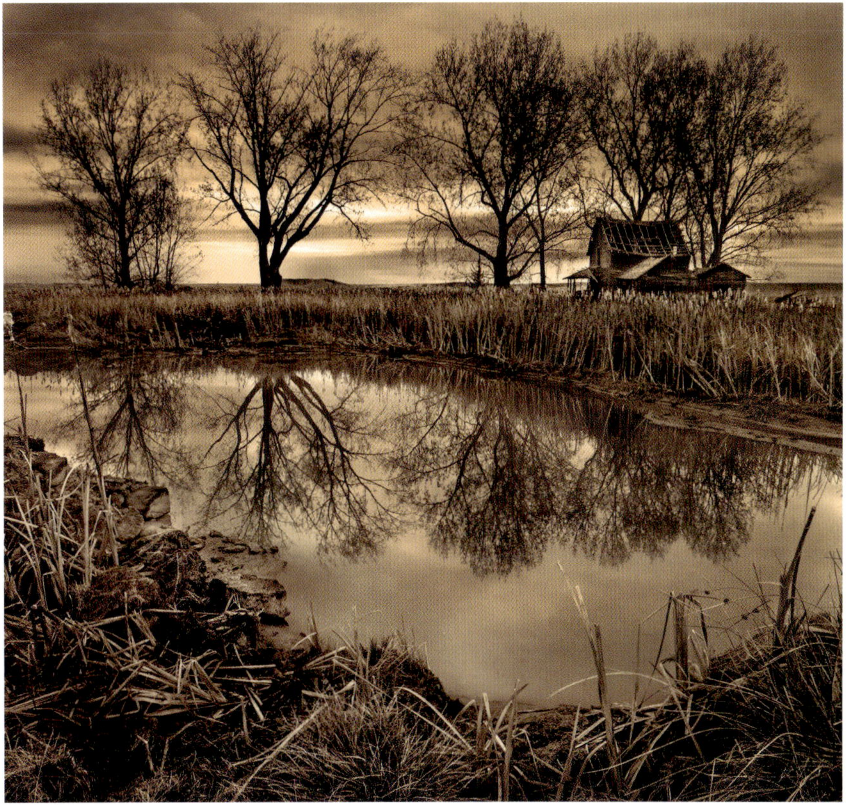

Alvord Desert. *Photo by John Kirk*

Farmhouse below Maupin. *Photo by Neal R. Thompson*

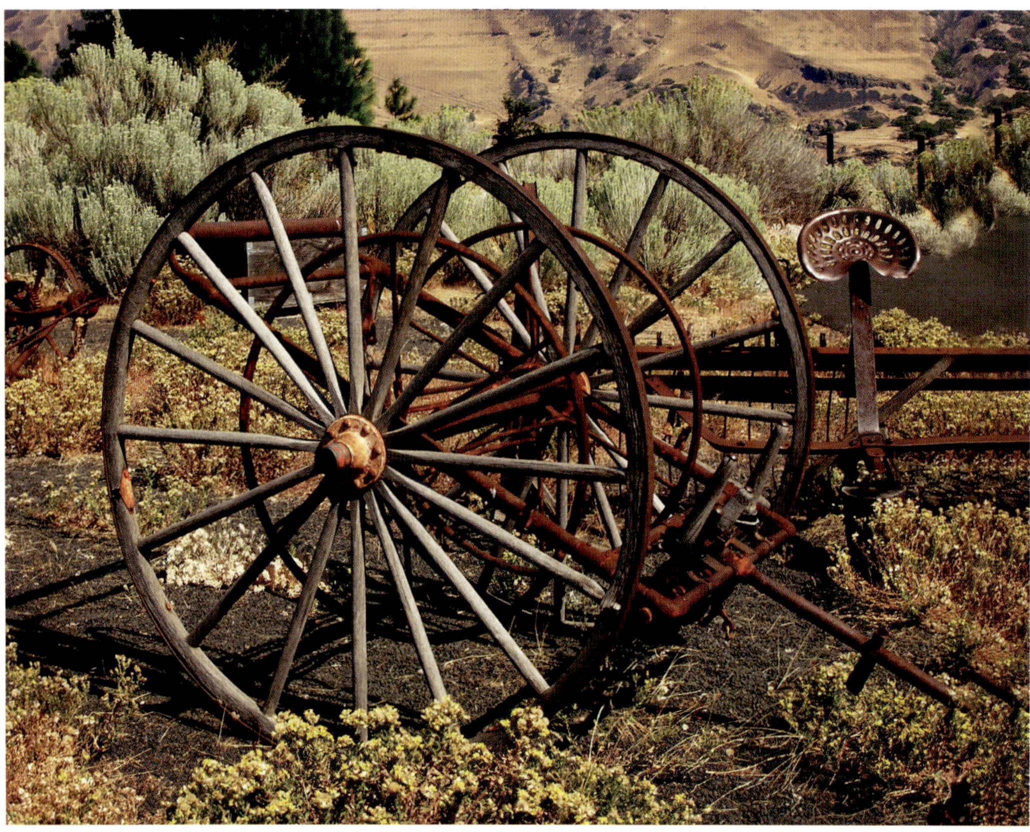

Old wagon wheel. *Photo by Andrea Shapiro*

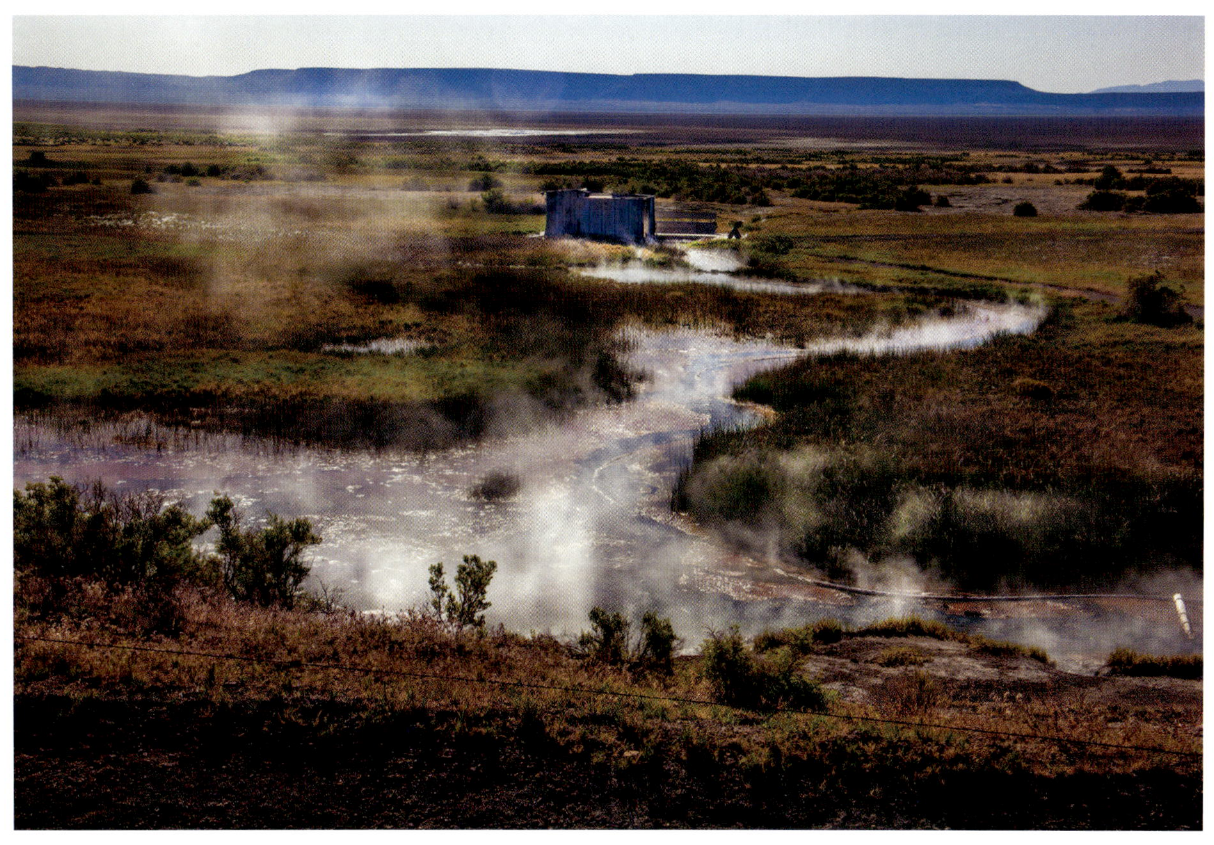

Alvord Hot Springs. *Photo by Neal R. Thompson*

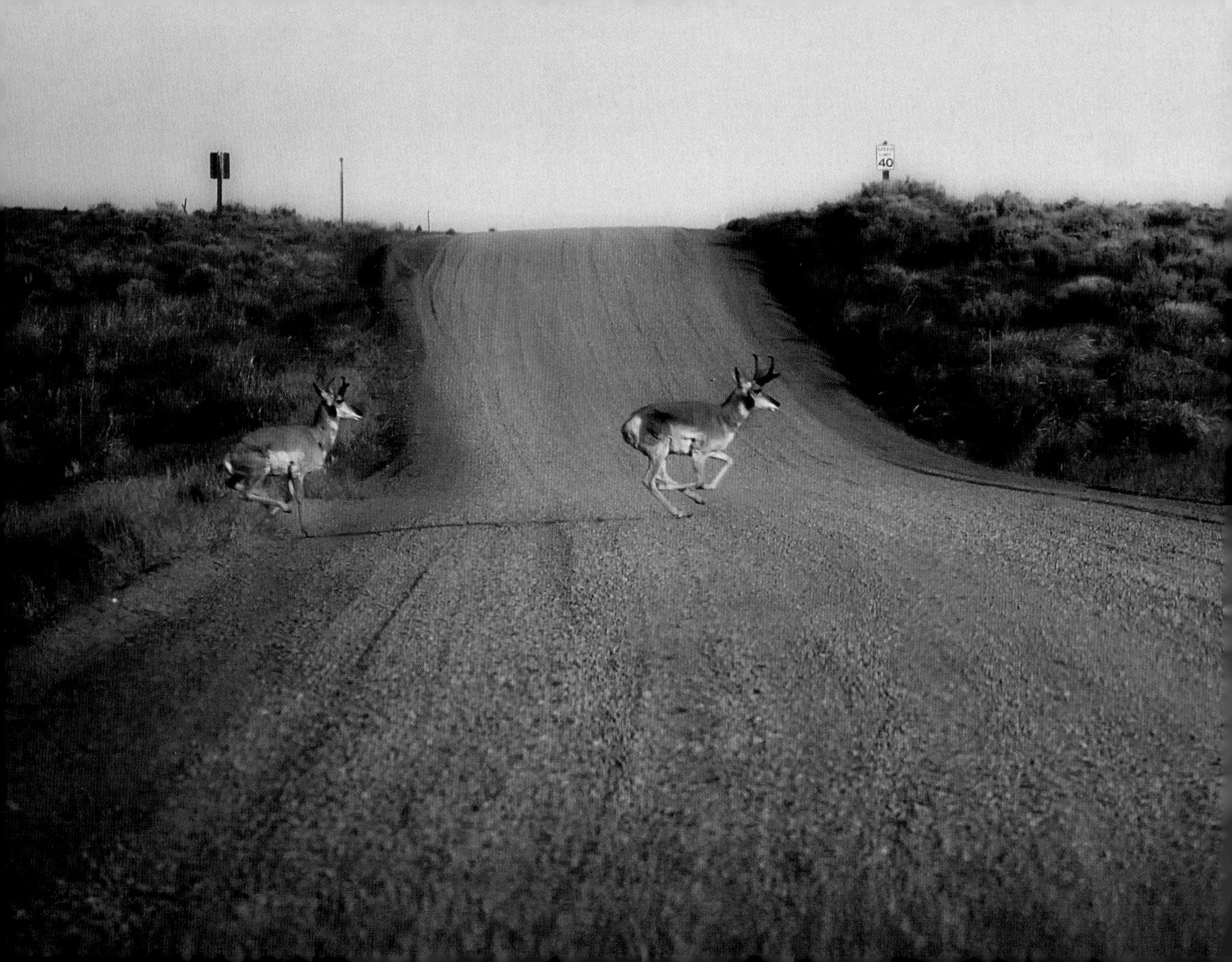
40

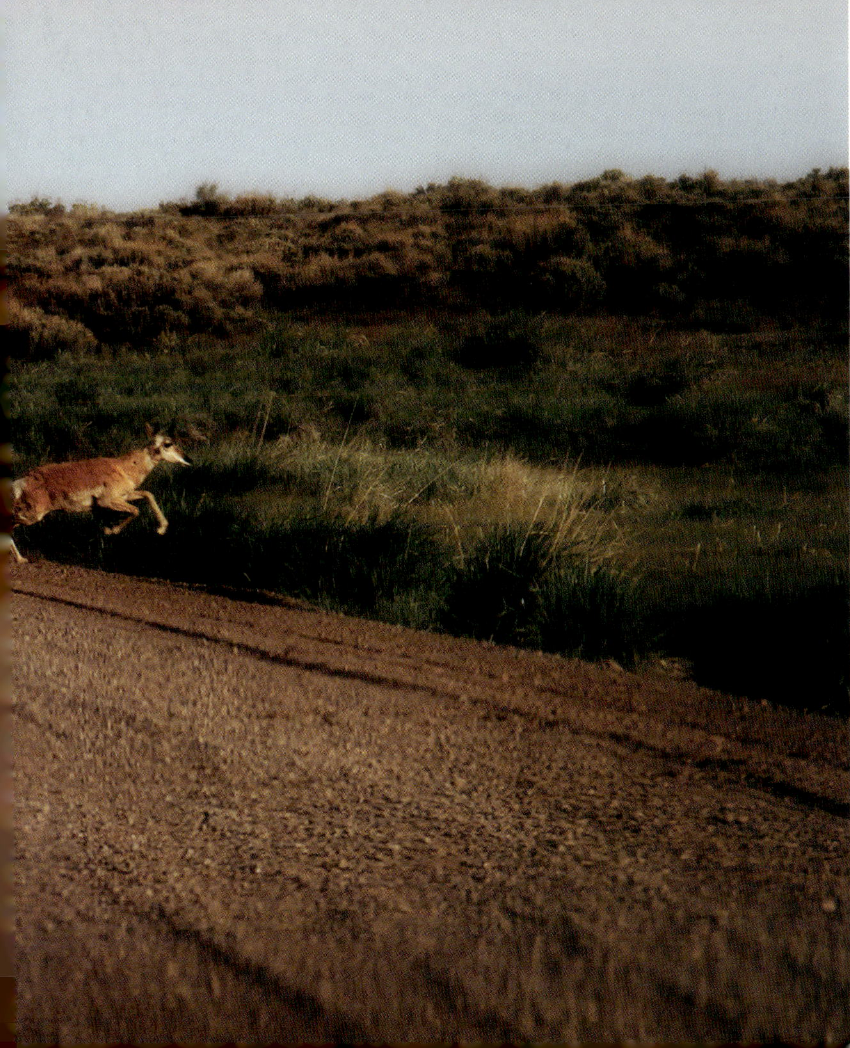

Pronghorn herd near Hart Mountain National Antelope Refuge.
Photo by John Kirk

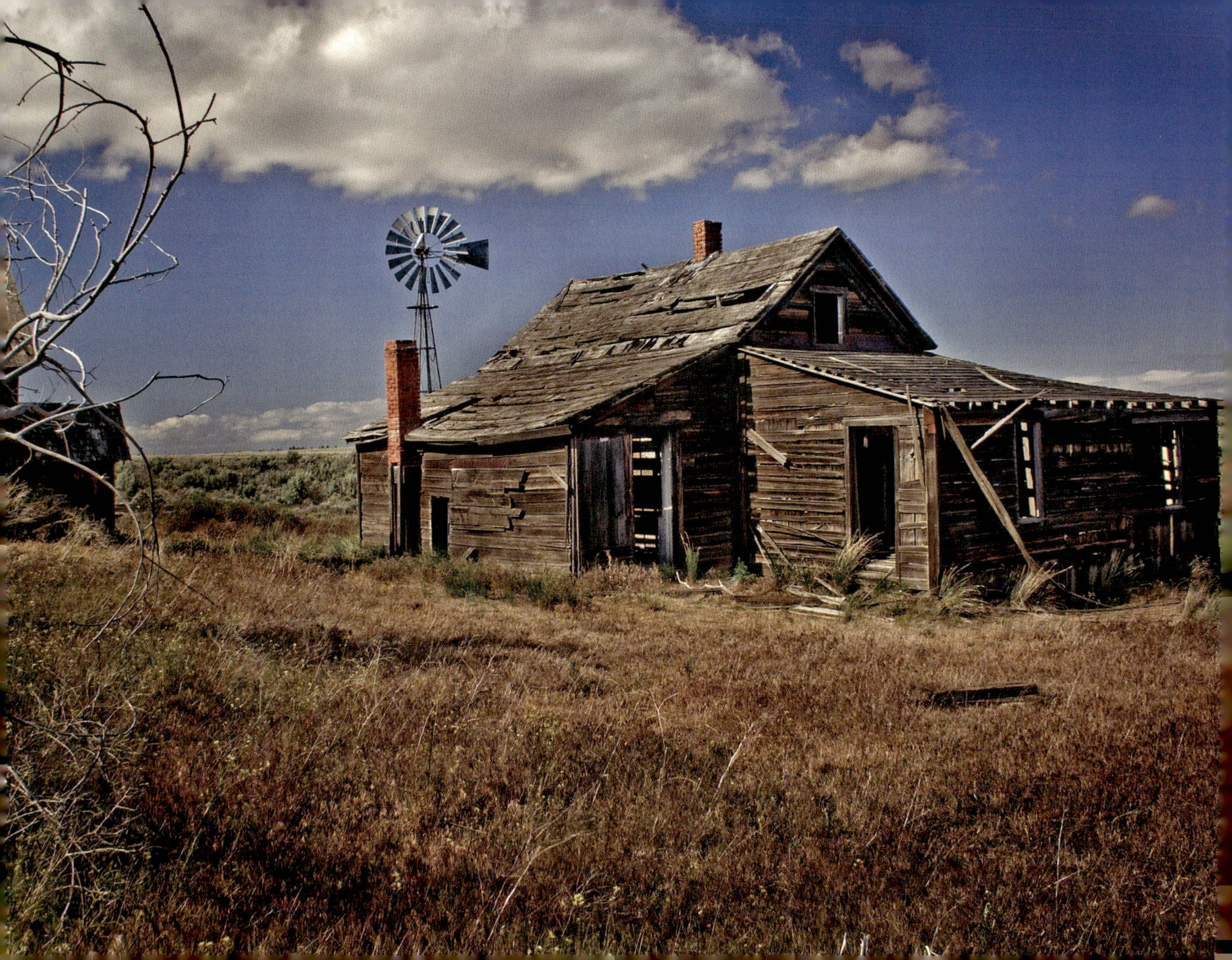

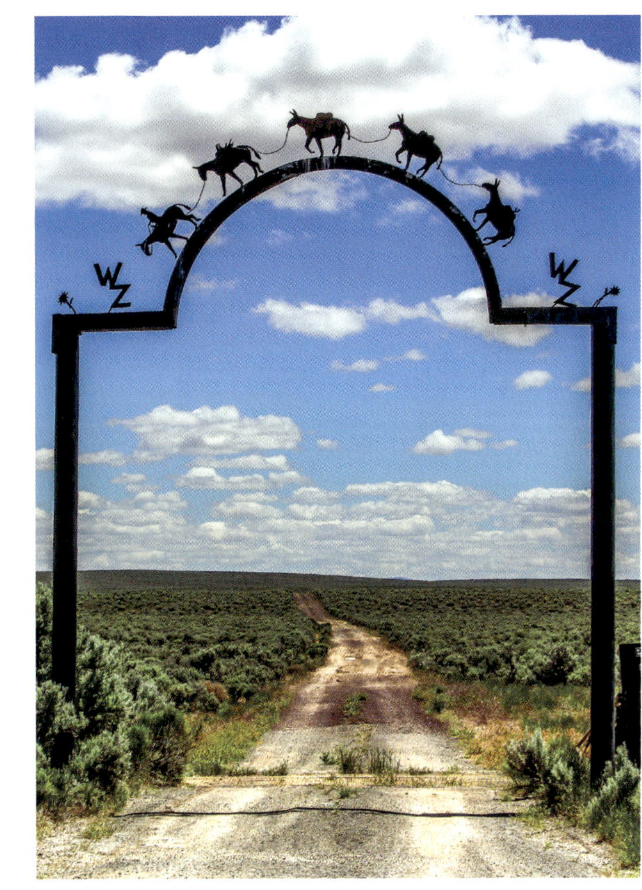

Farmhouse near Kent. *Photo by Neal R. Thompson*

Ranch entry near Diamond. *Photo by Terry Fisher*

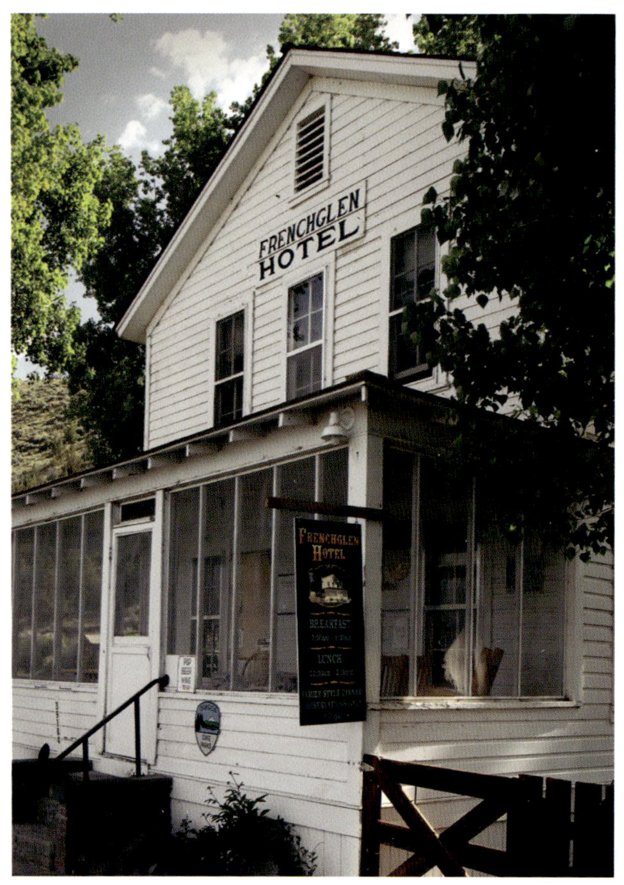

Frenchglen Hotel, Steens Mountain. Situated in the tiny town of Frenchglen (population twelve), this hotel was built in 1924. *Photo by John Kirk*

Geiser Grand Hotel, Baker City. Once the finest hotel between Portland and Salt Lake City, this hotel, built in 1893, is said to be haunted. *Photo by Terry Fisher*

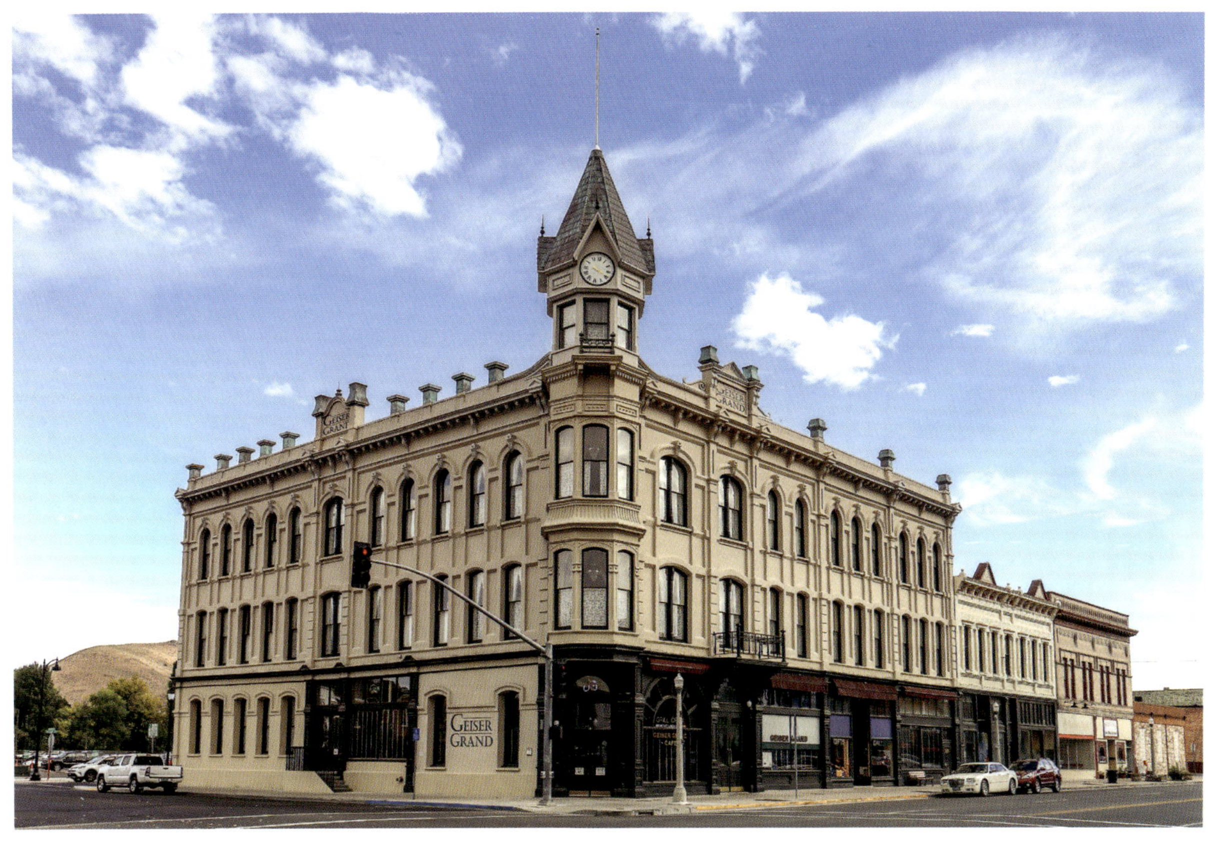
GEISER
GRAND

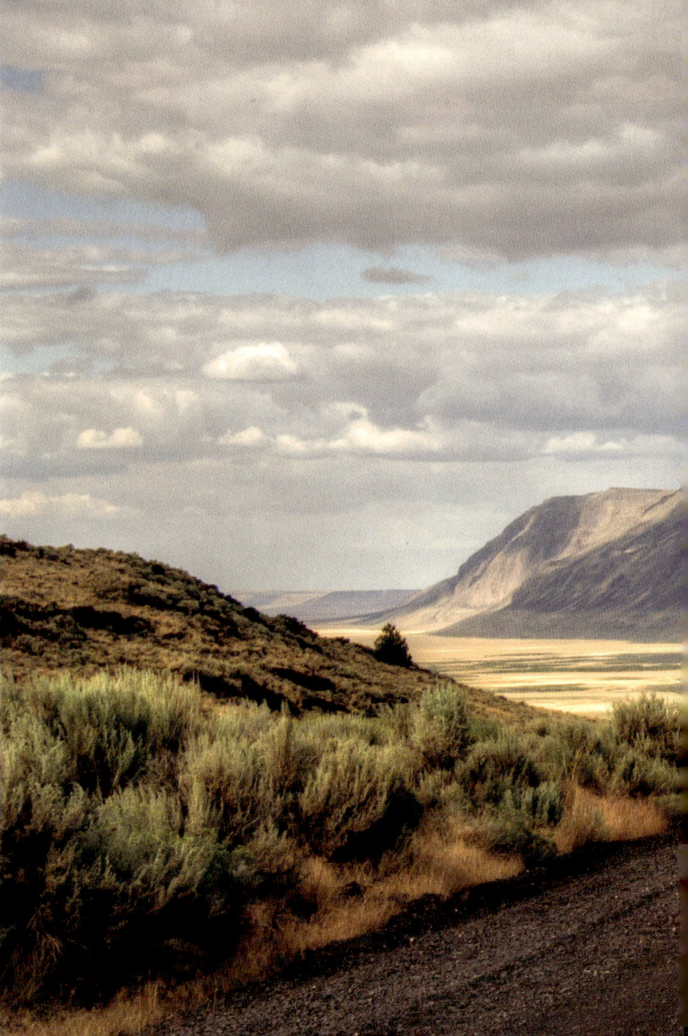

Hart Mountain. *Photo by Sue Newman*

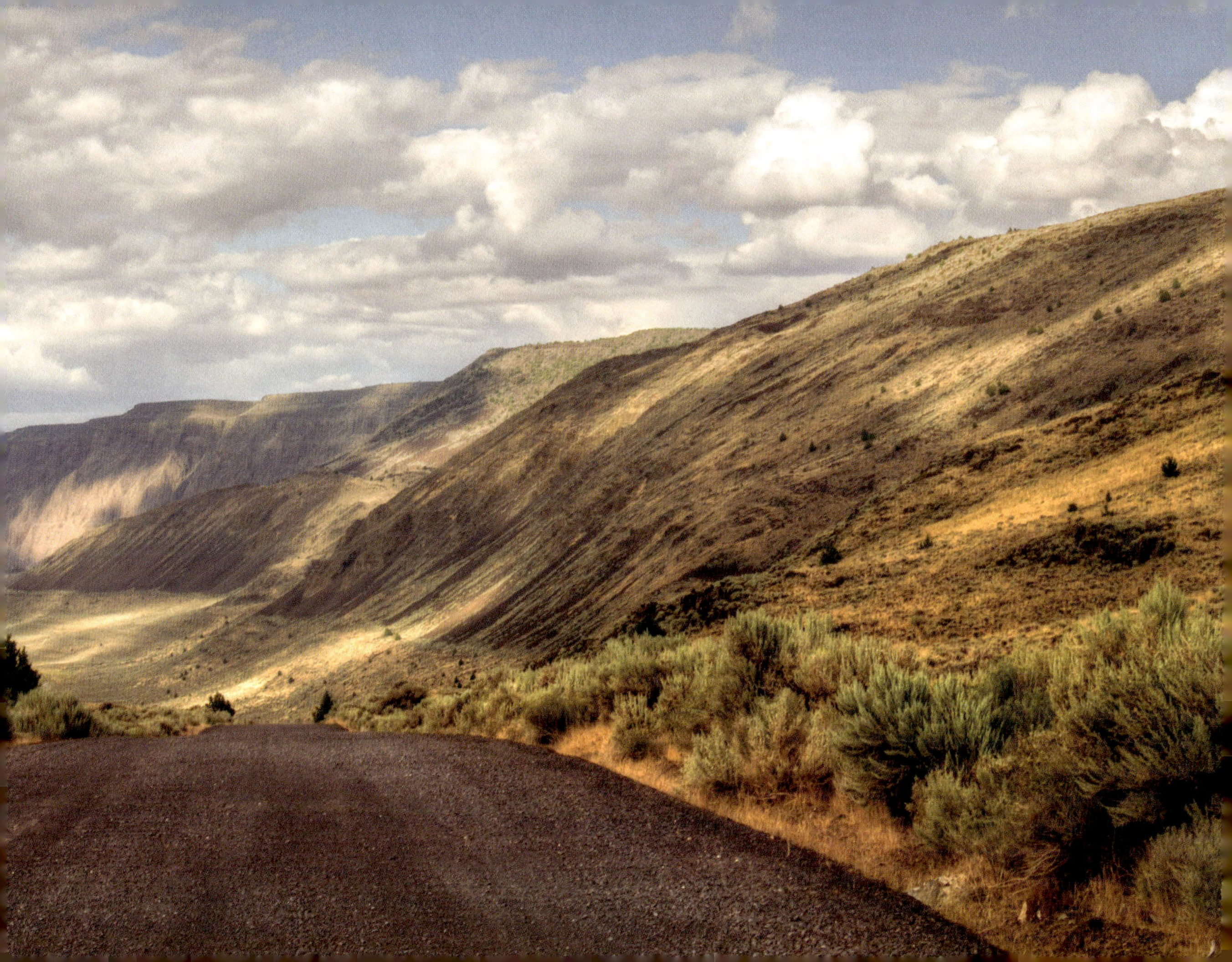

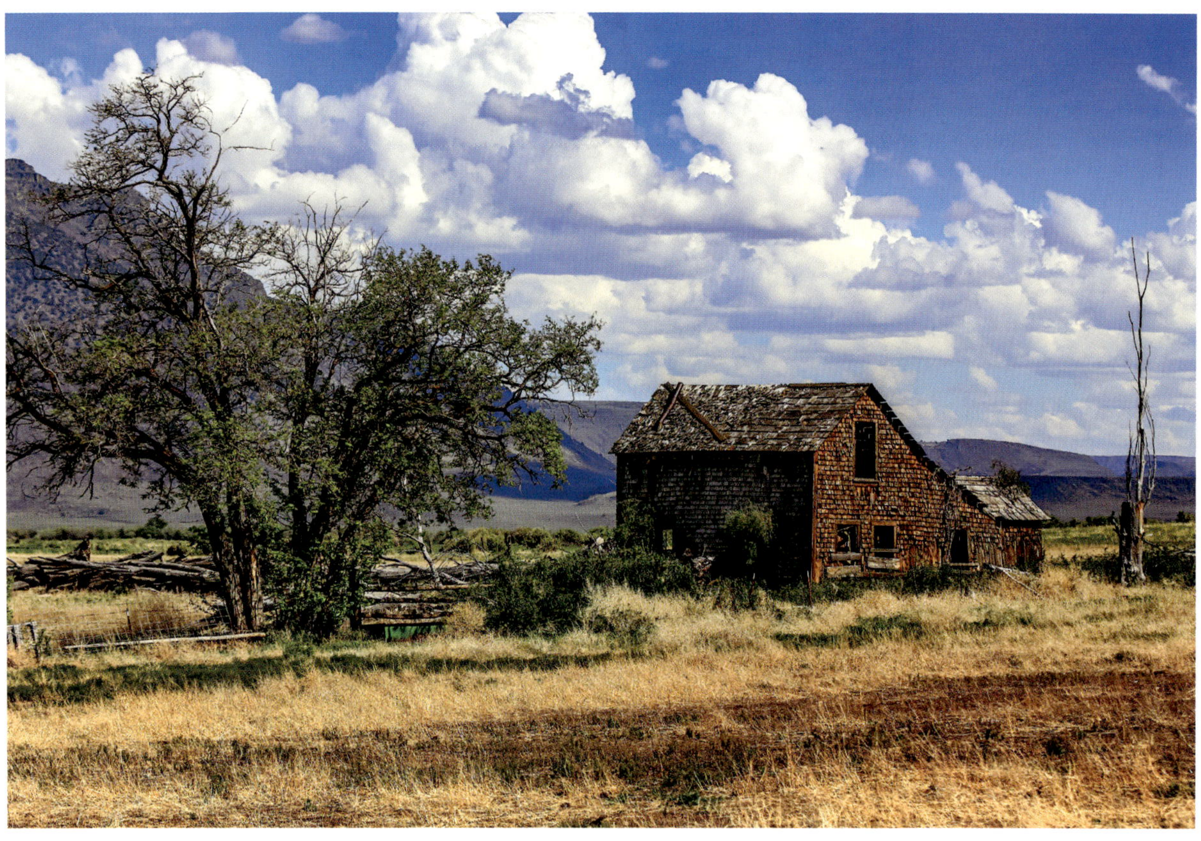

Abandoned building, Plush. *Photo by Terry Fisher*

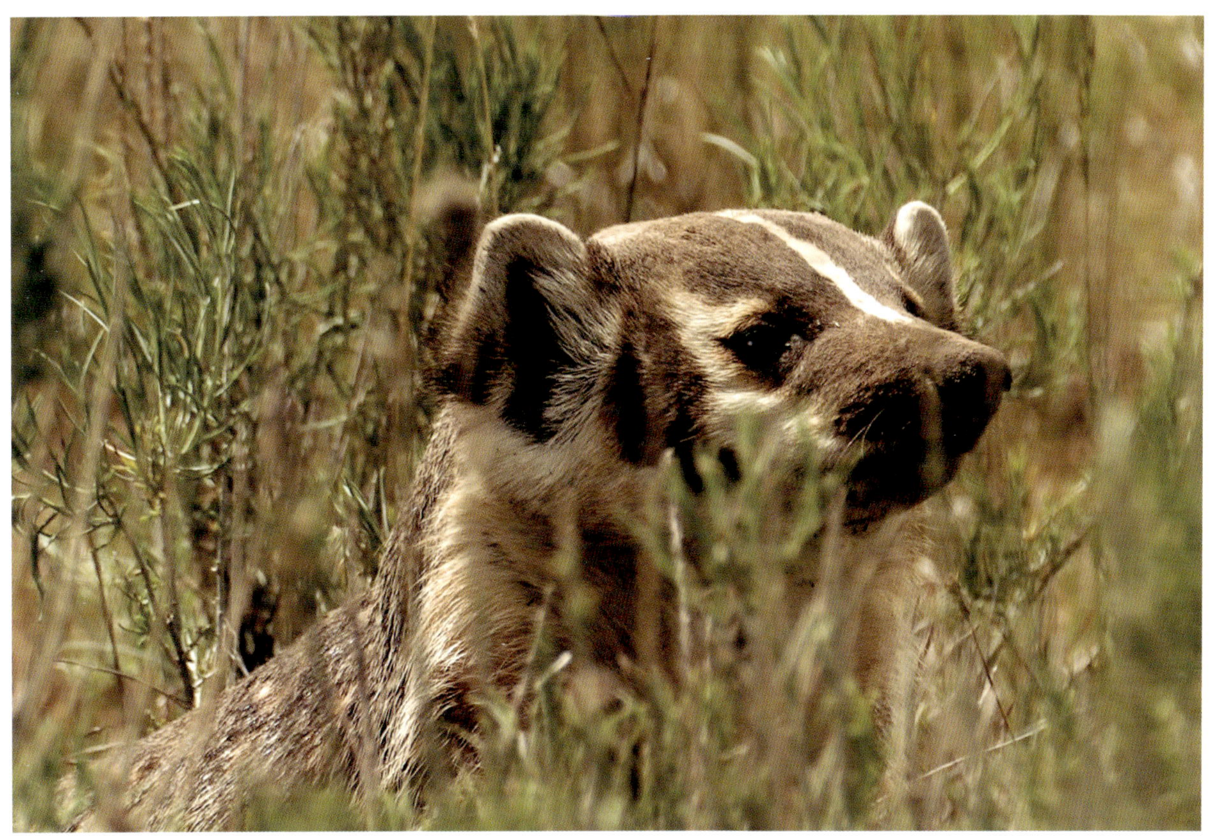

Badger, Malheur National Wildlife Refuge.
Photo by George F. Peterson

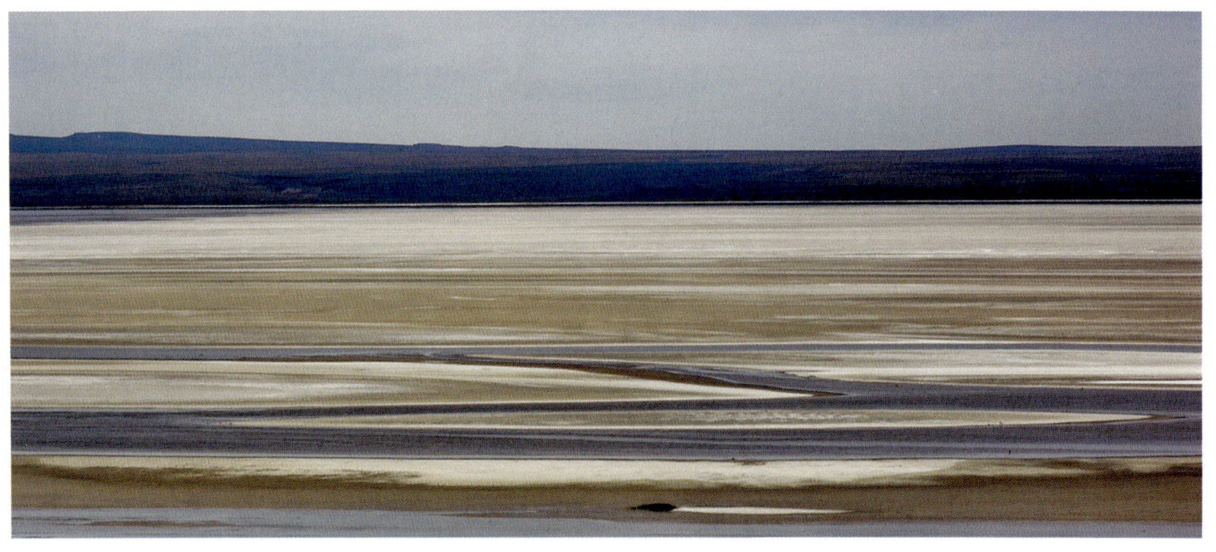

Lake Abert. *Photo by Vivian McAleavey*

Christmas Valley. *Photo by Nomeca Hartwell*

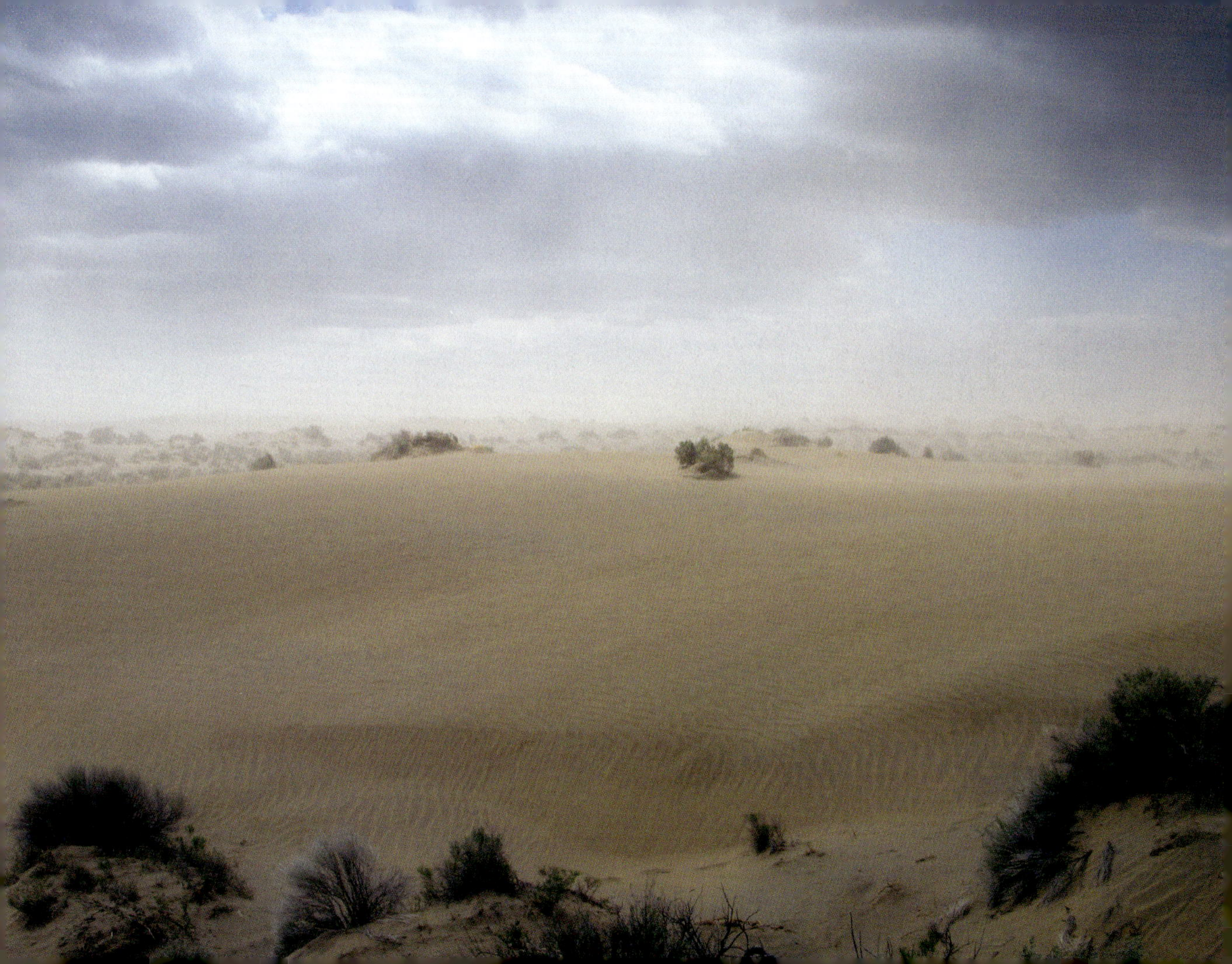

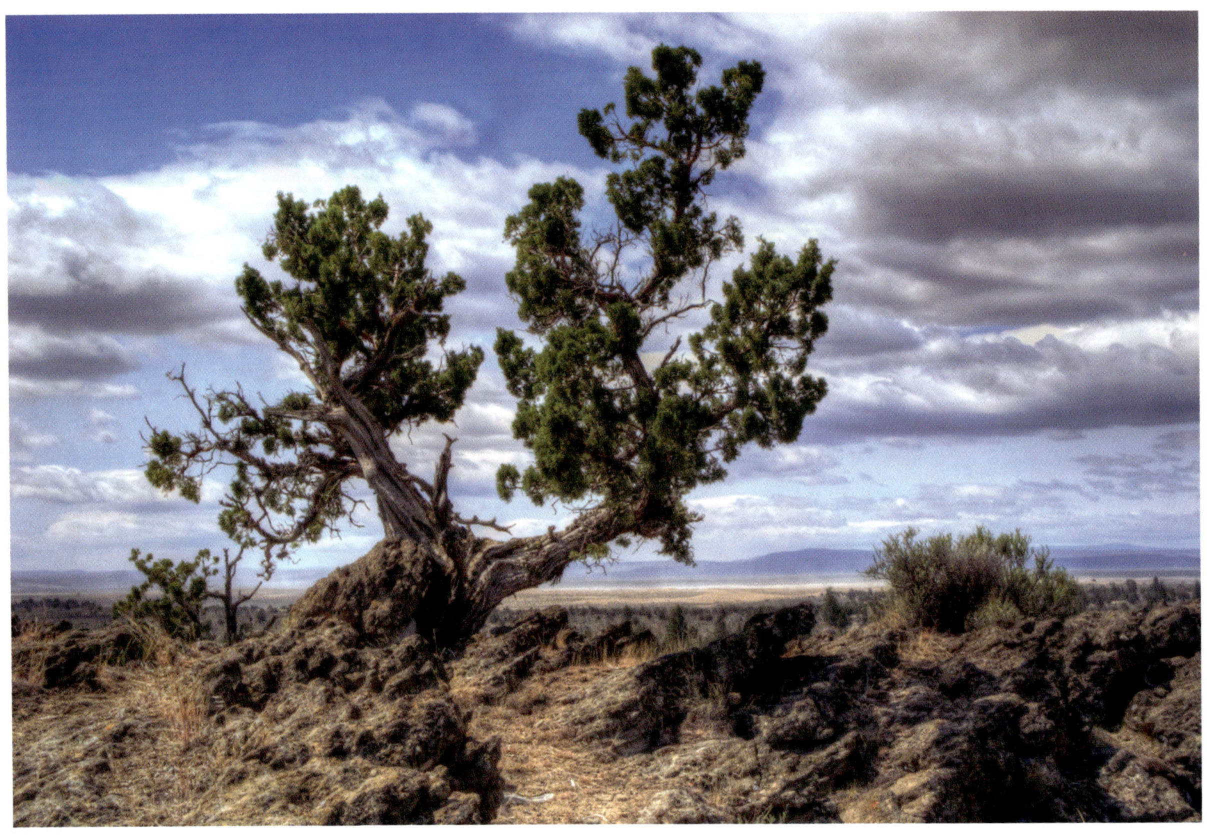

Christmas Valley. *Photo by Nomeca Hartwell*

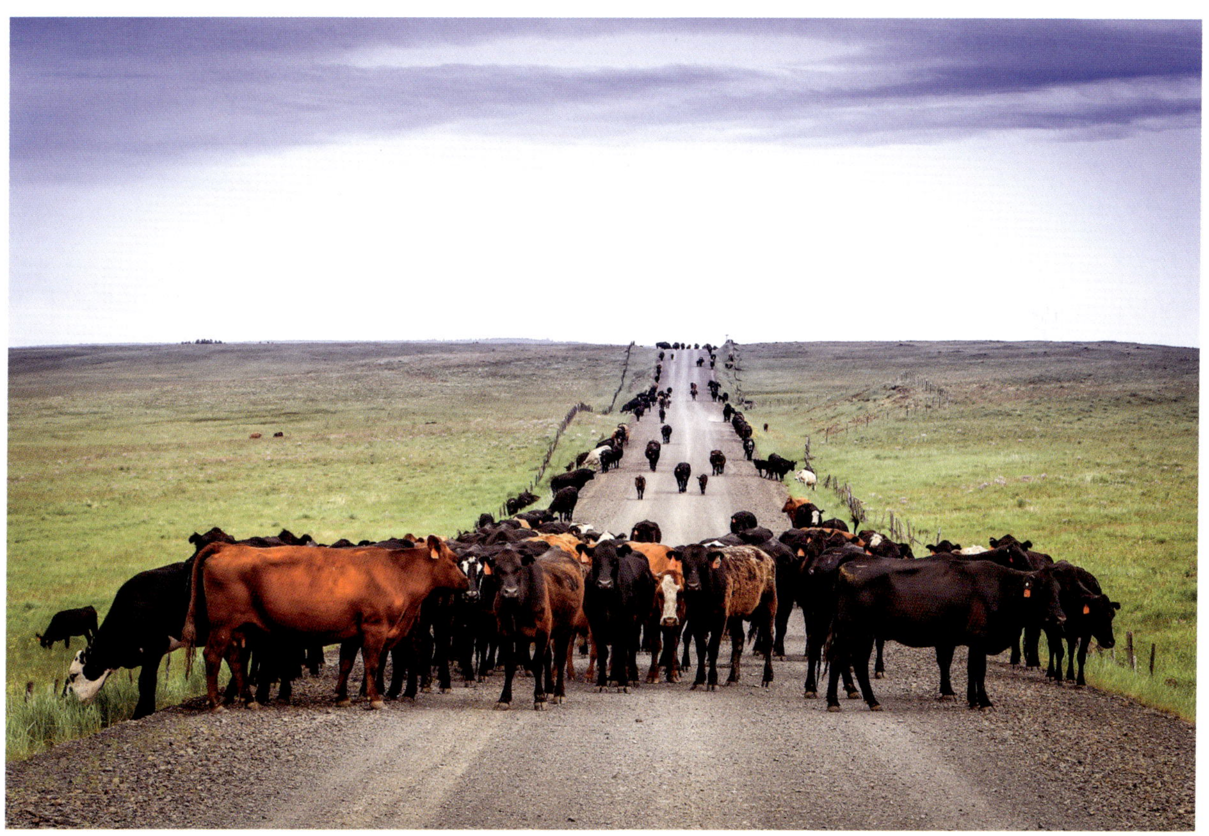

Cattle drive on Zumwalt Prairie Road, near Joseph.
Photo by Terry Fisher

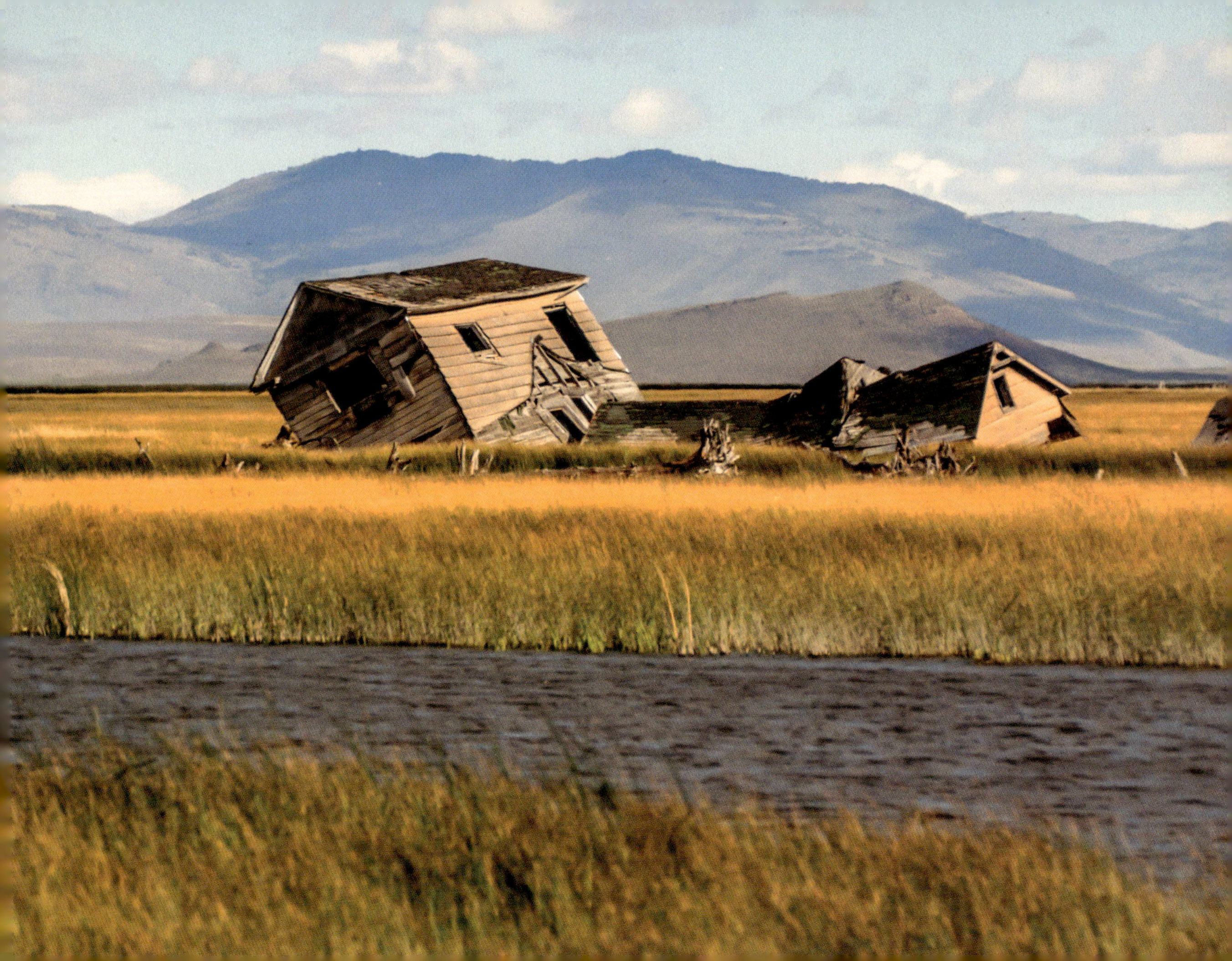

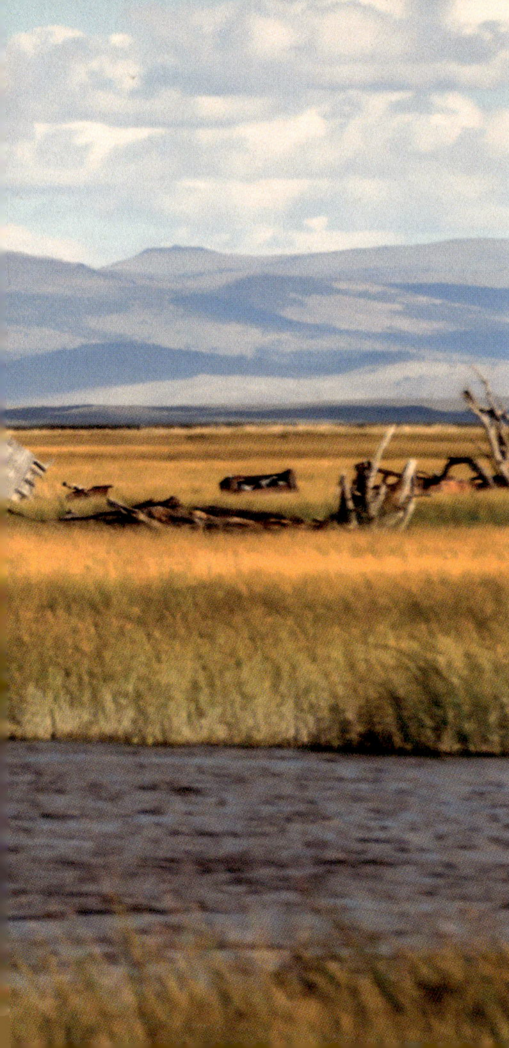

Abandoned buildings near Malheur National Wildlife Refuge.
Photo by George F. Peterson

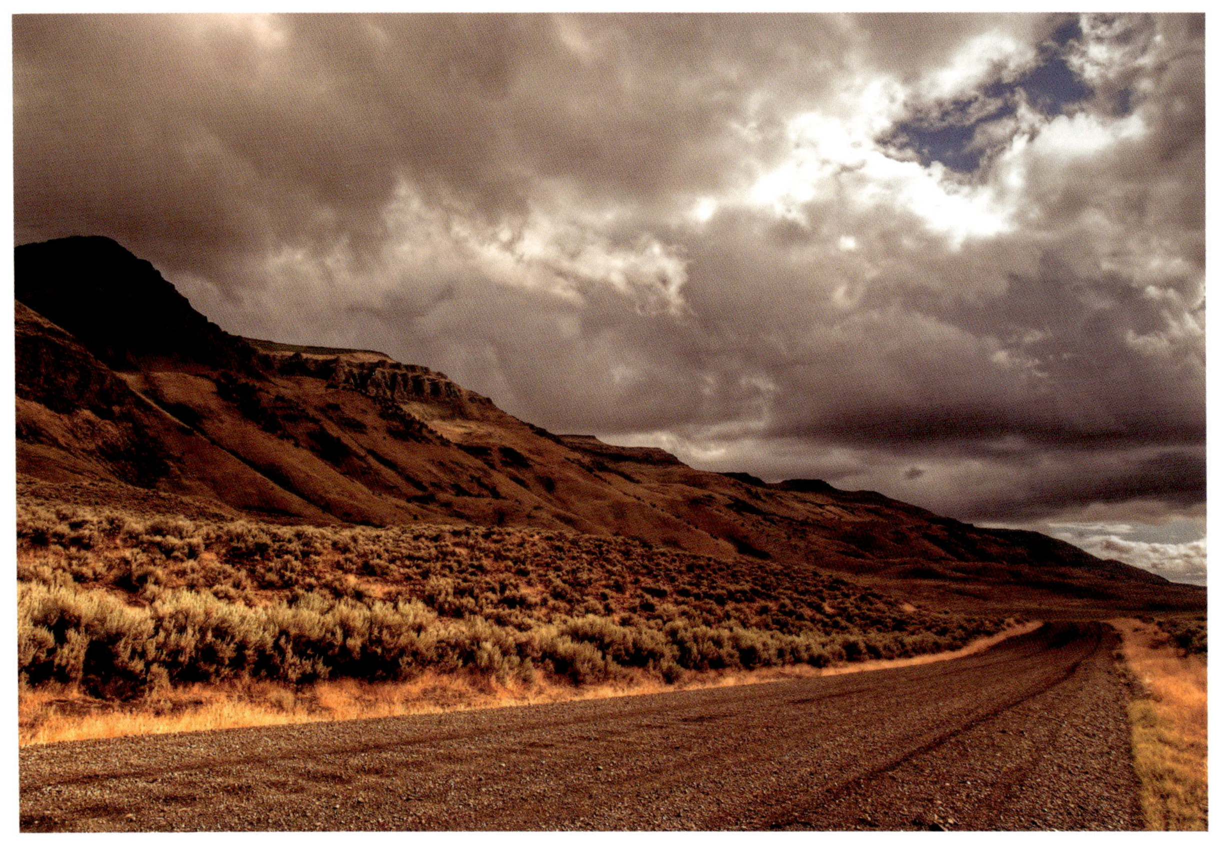

Hart Mountain. *Photo by Sue Newman*

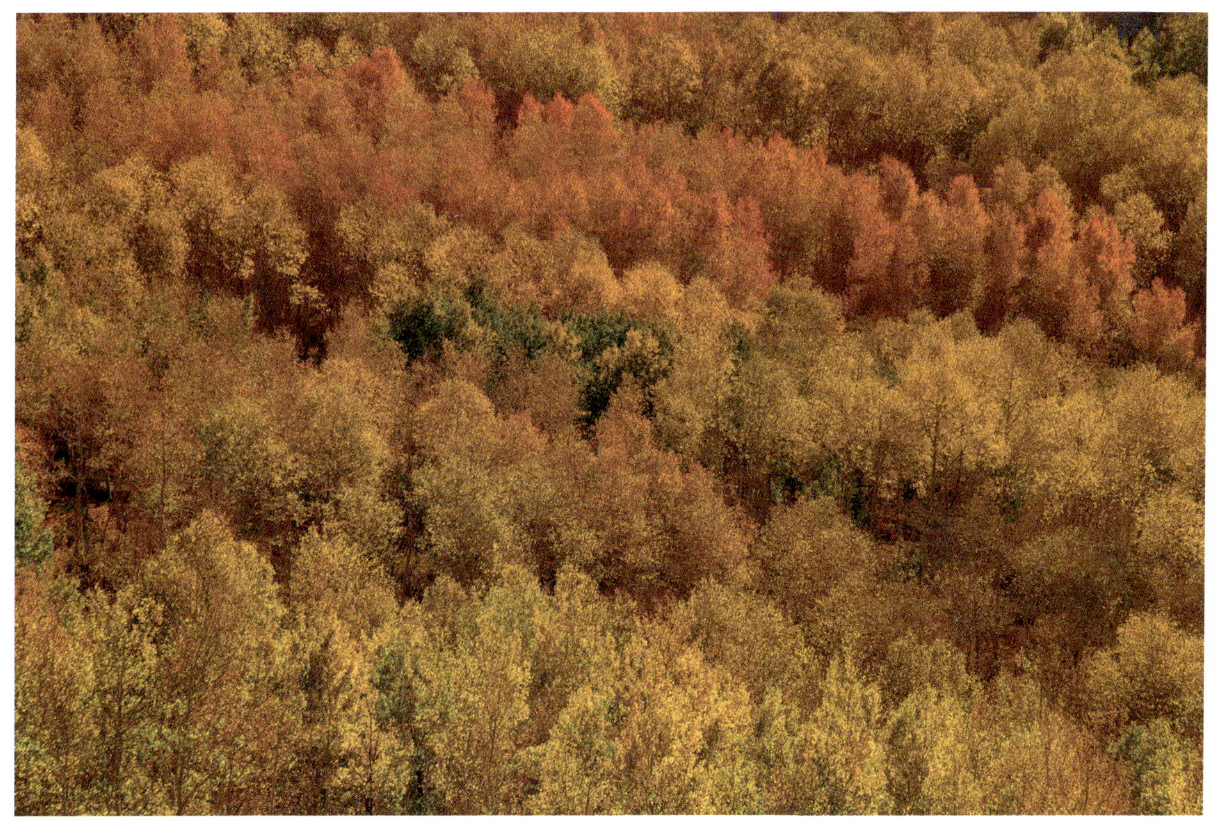

Steens Mountain fall colors. *Photo by Clem Paslack*

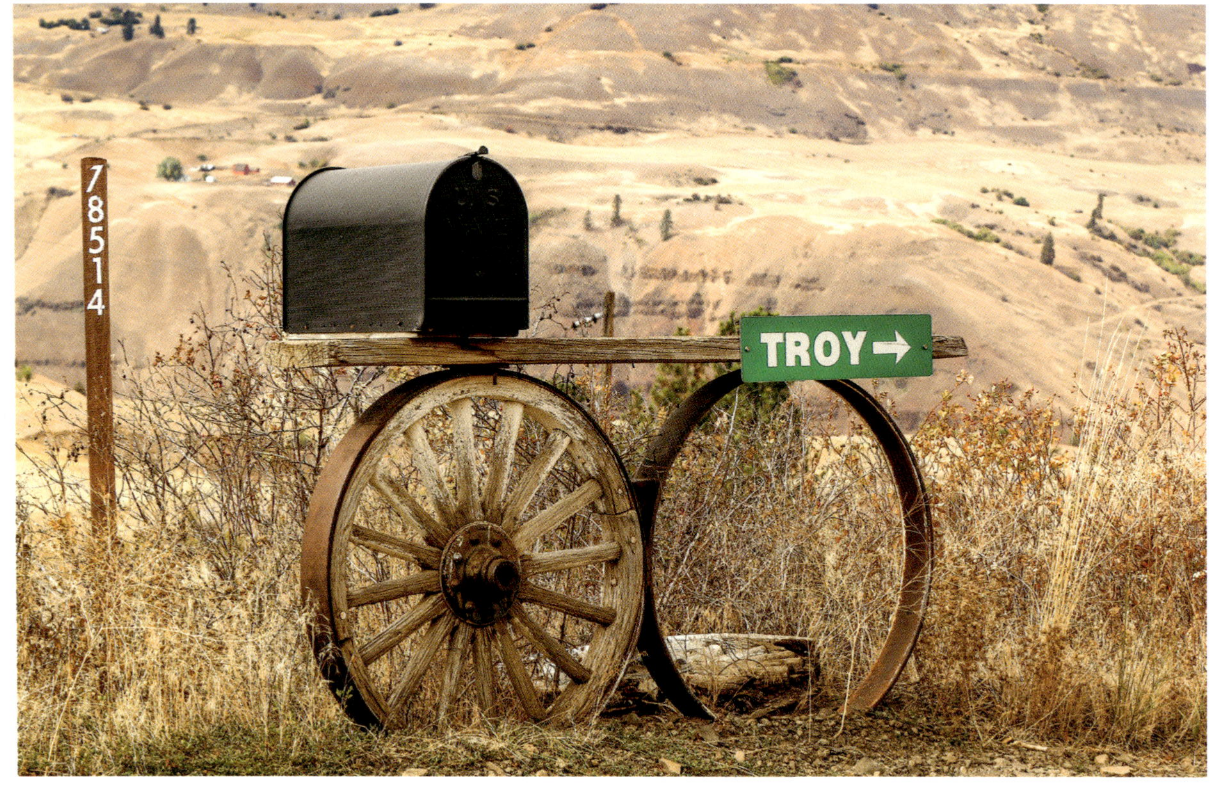

Rural mailbox near Troy. *Photo by Terry Fisher*

Cowboy on Route 205, Malheur. *Photo by George F. Peterson*

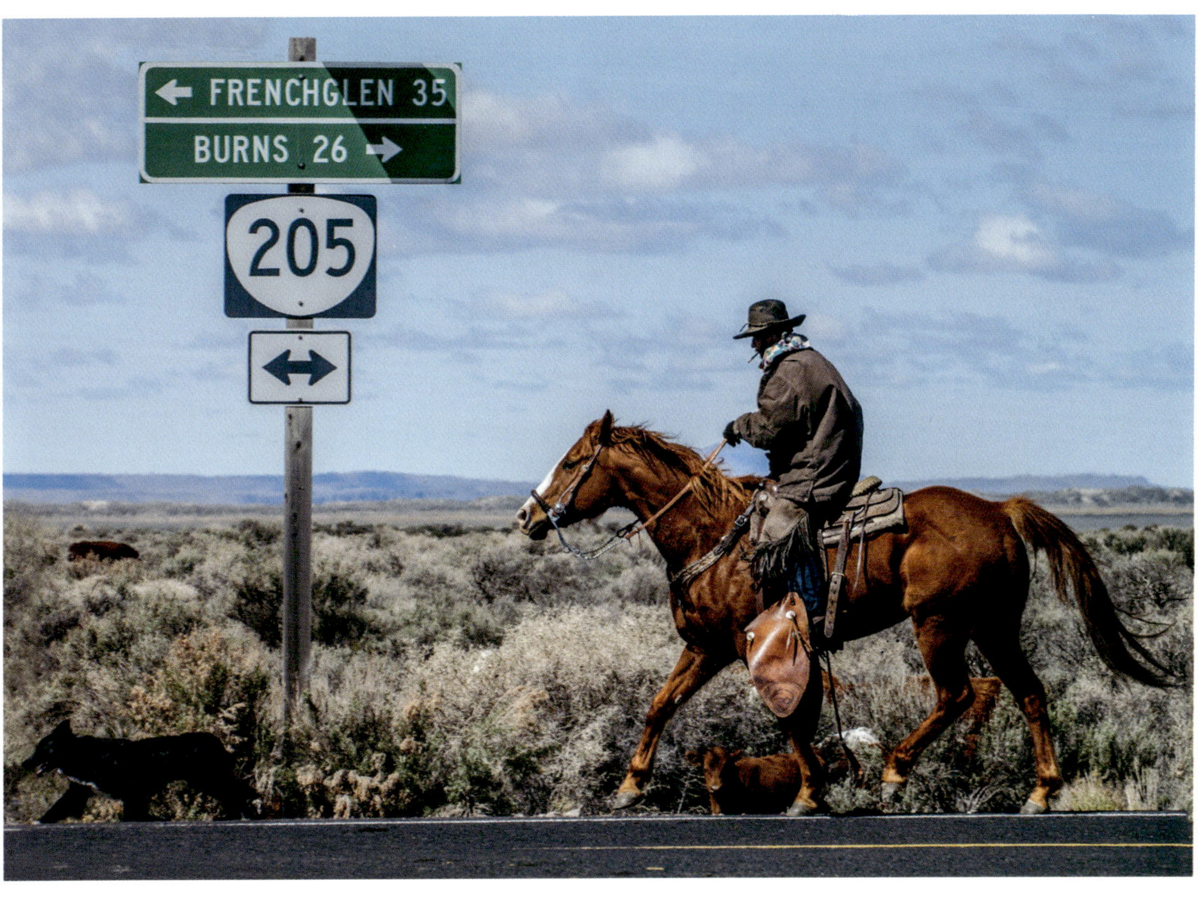
← FRENCHGLEN 35
BURNS 26 →
205

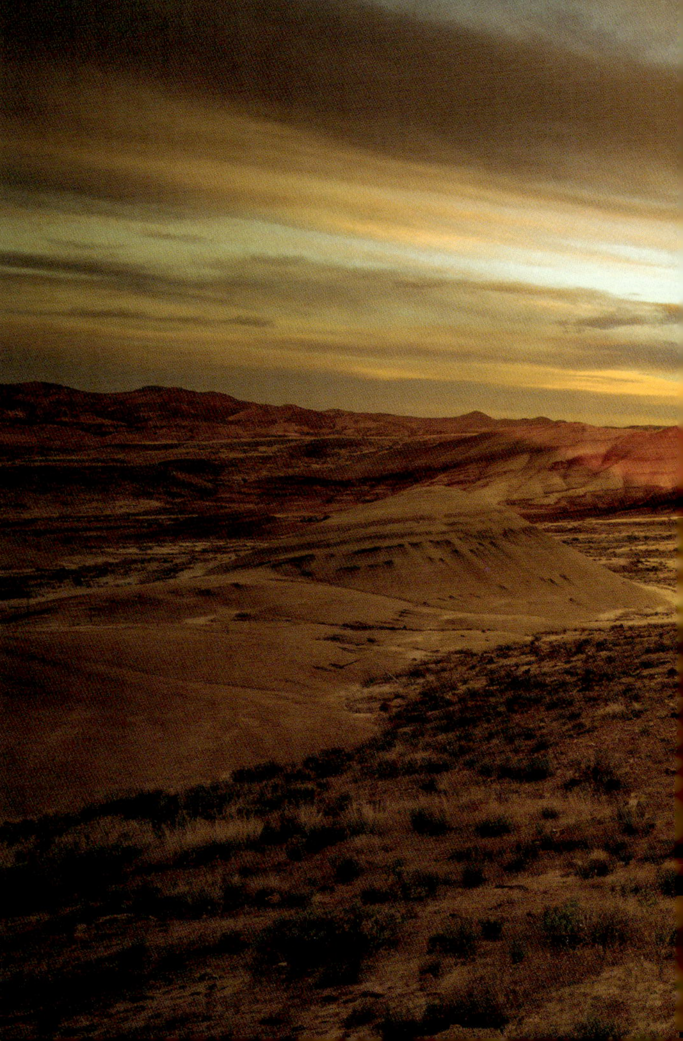

Painted Hills. *Photo by Alana Lynn Starkweather*

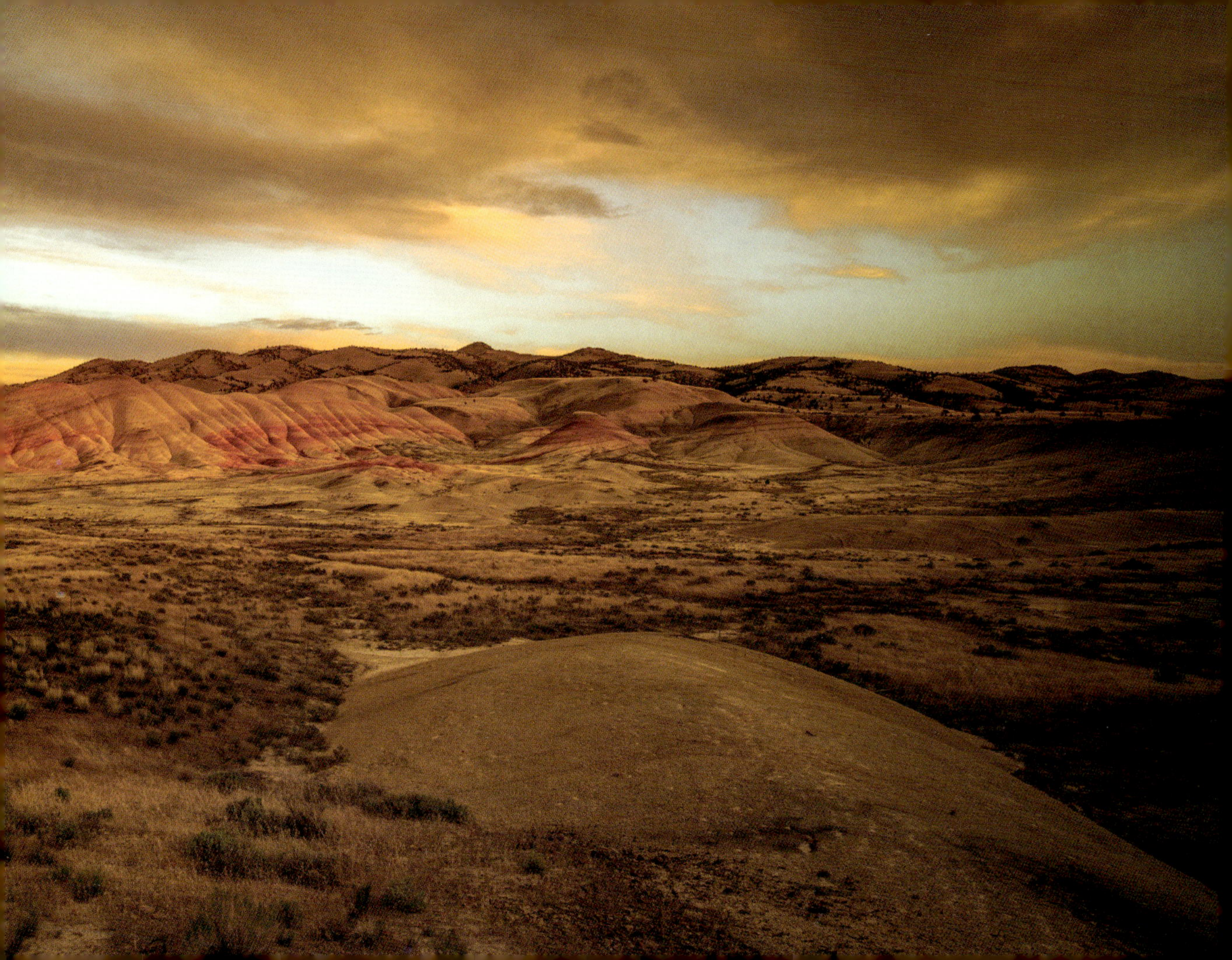

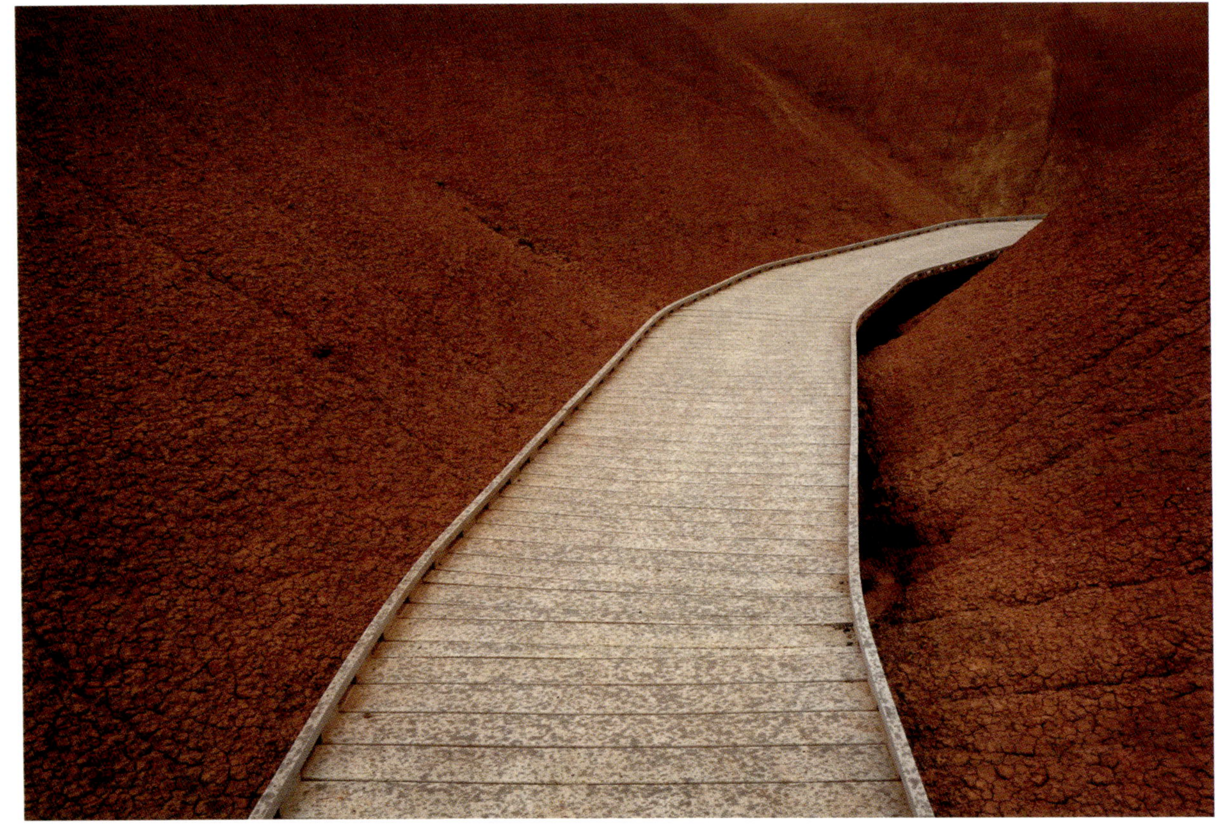

John Day Fossil Beds National Monument boardwalk at Painted Cove Overlook. *Photo by John Kirk*

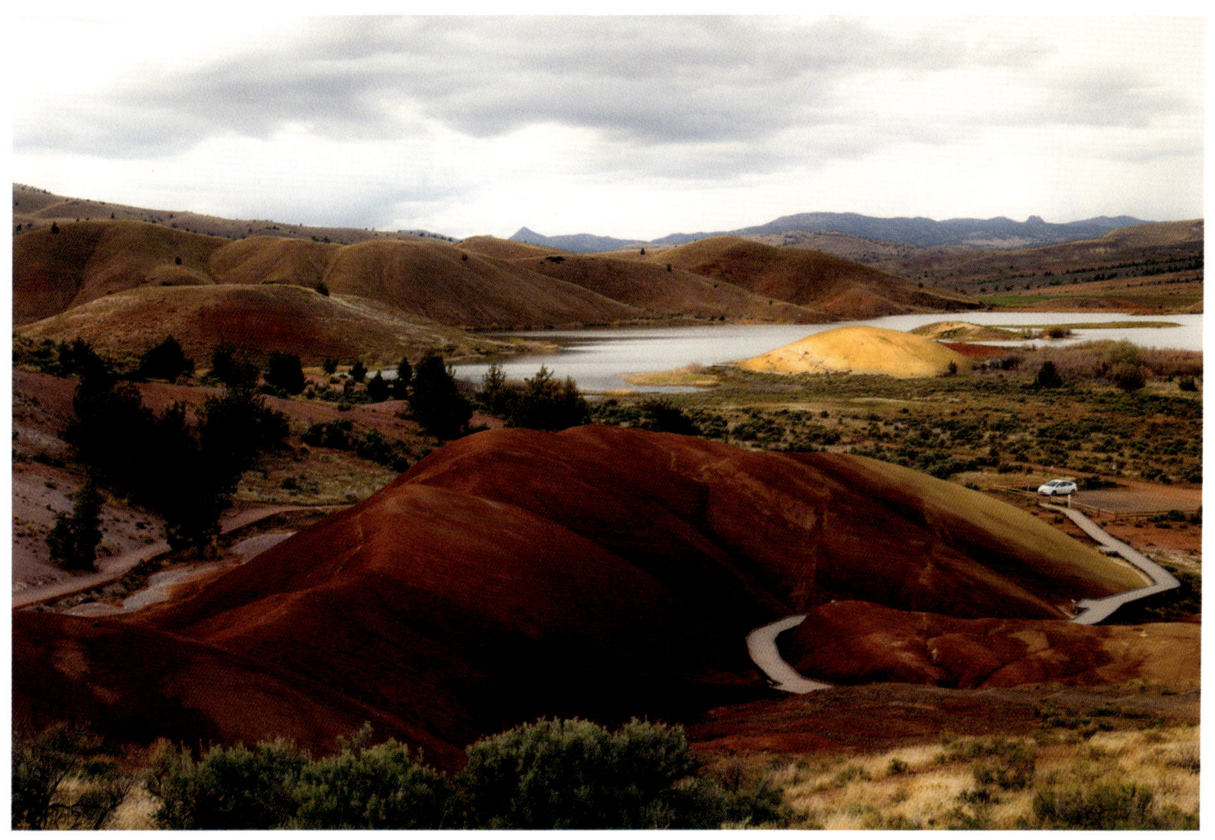

Painted Cove Overlook Trail, John Day Fossil Beds National Monument. *Photo by Nomeca Hartwell*

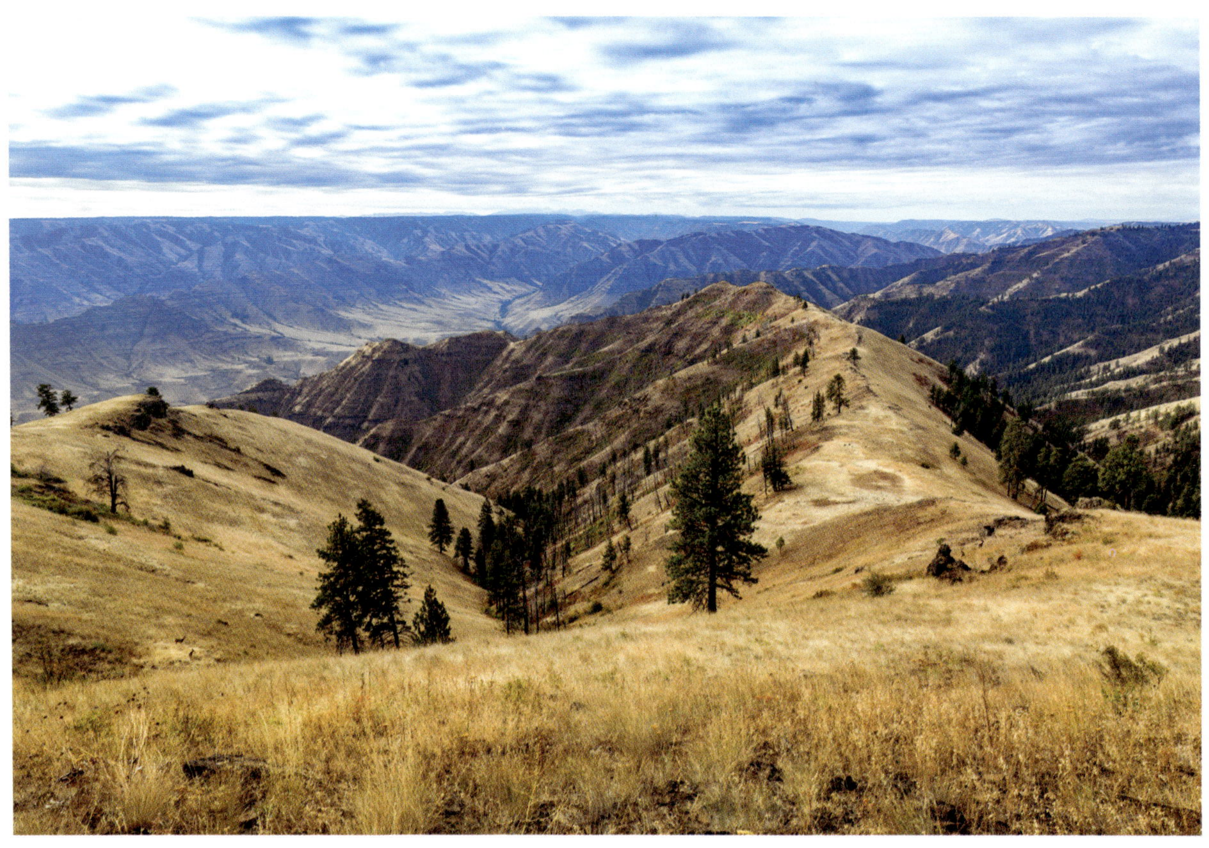

Buckhorn Overlook, Zumwalt Prairie. *Photo by Nick Viani*

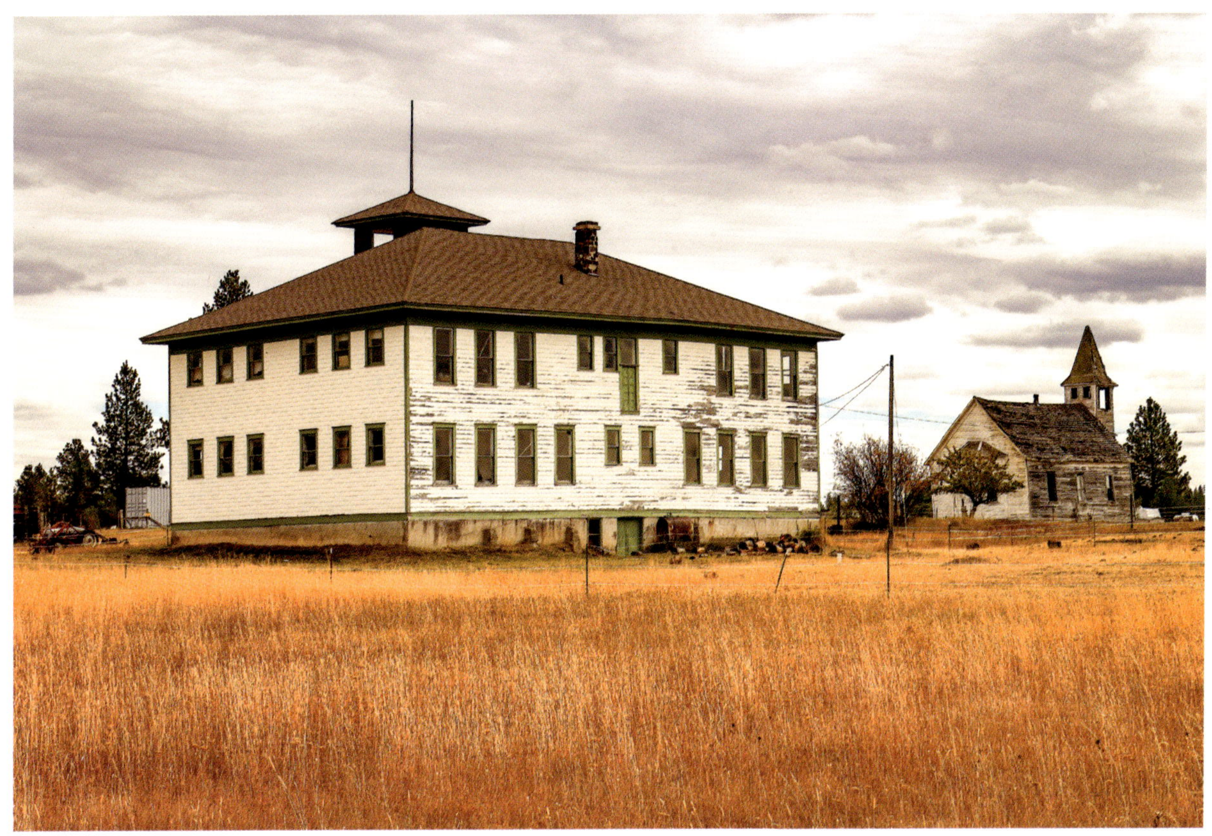

Historical school in the ghost town of Flora. *Photo by Terry Fisher*

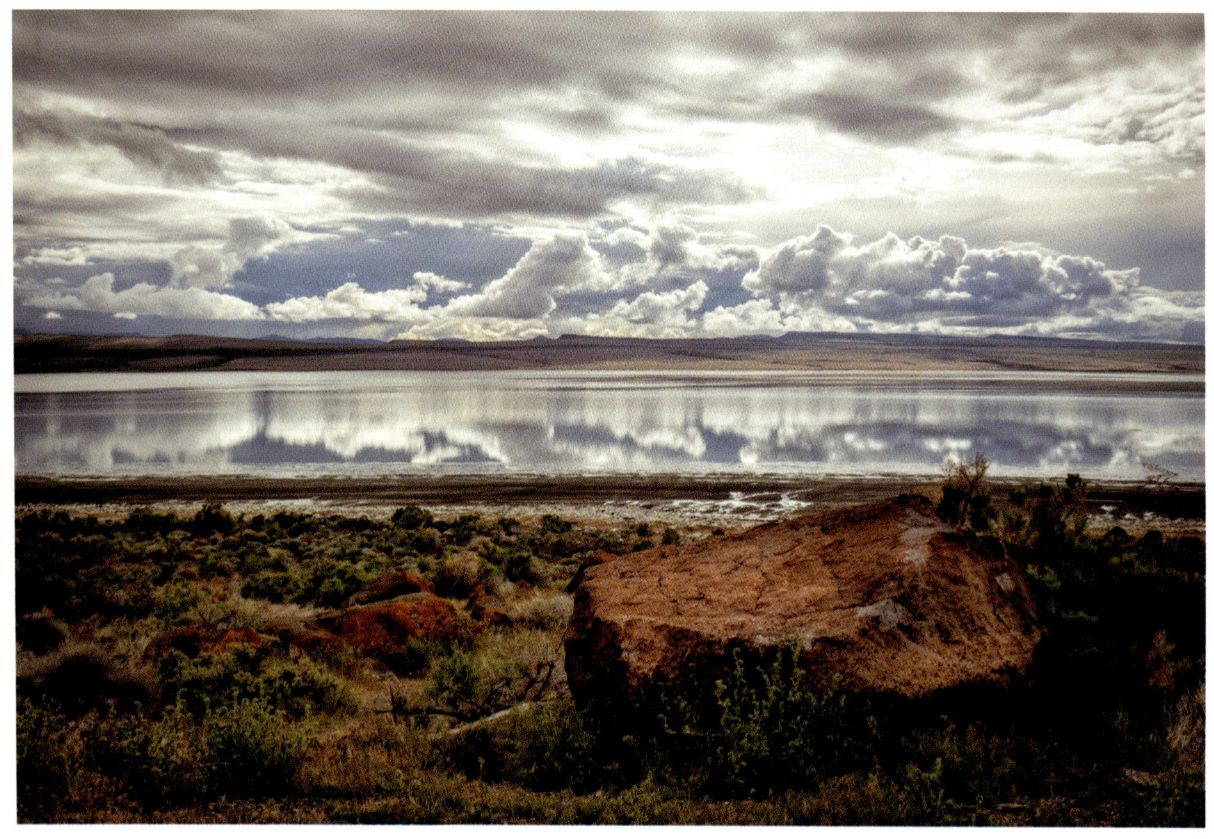

Lake Abert. *Photo by Barbara Tricarico*

Alvord Desert. *Photo by Diana Standing*

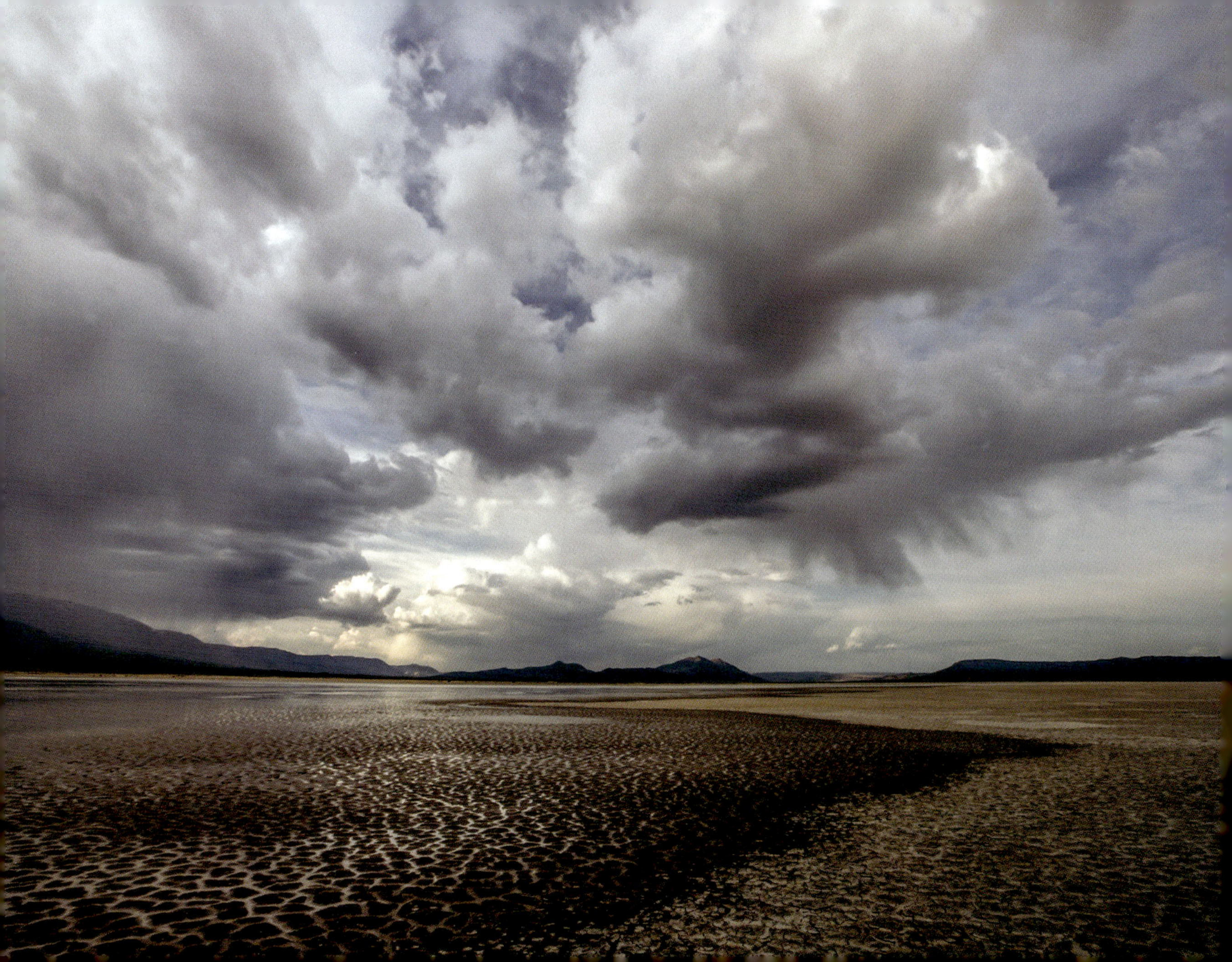

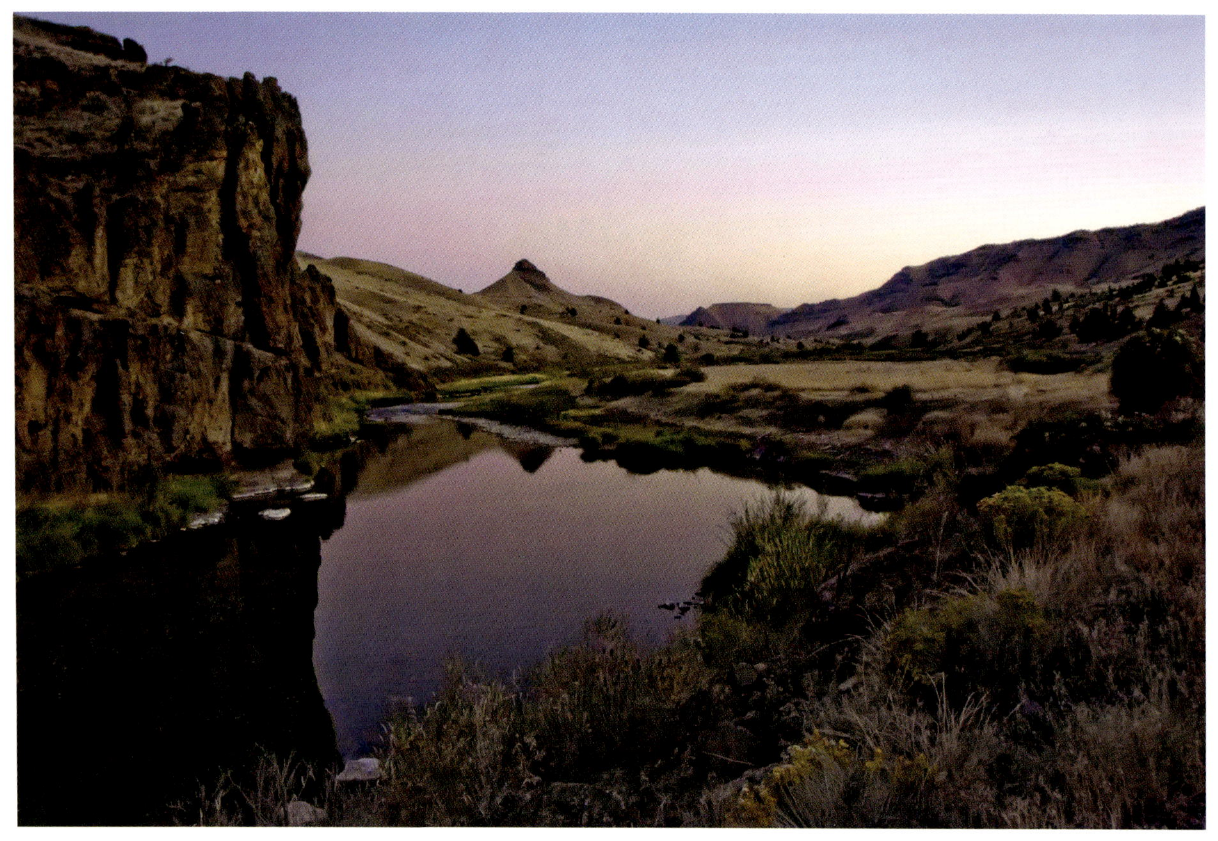

John Day River at dusk, John Day Fossil Beds National Monument.
Photo by Matt Witt

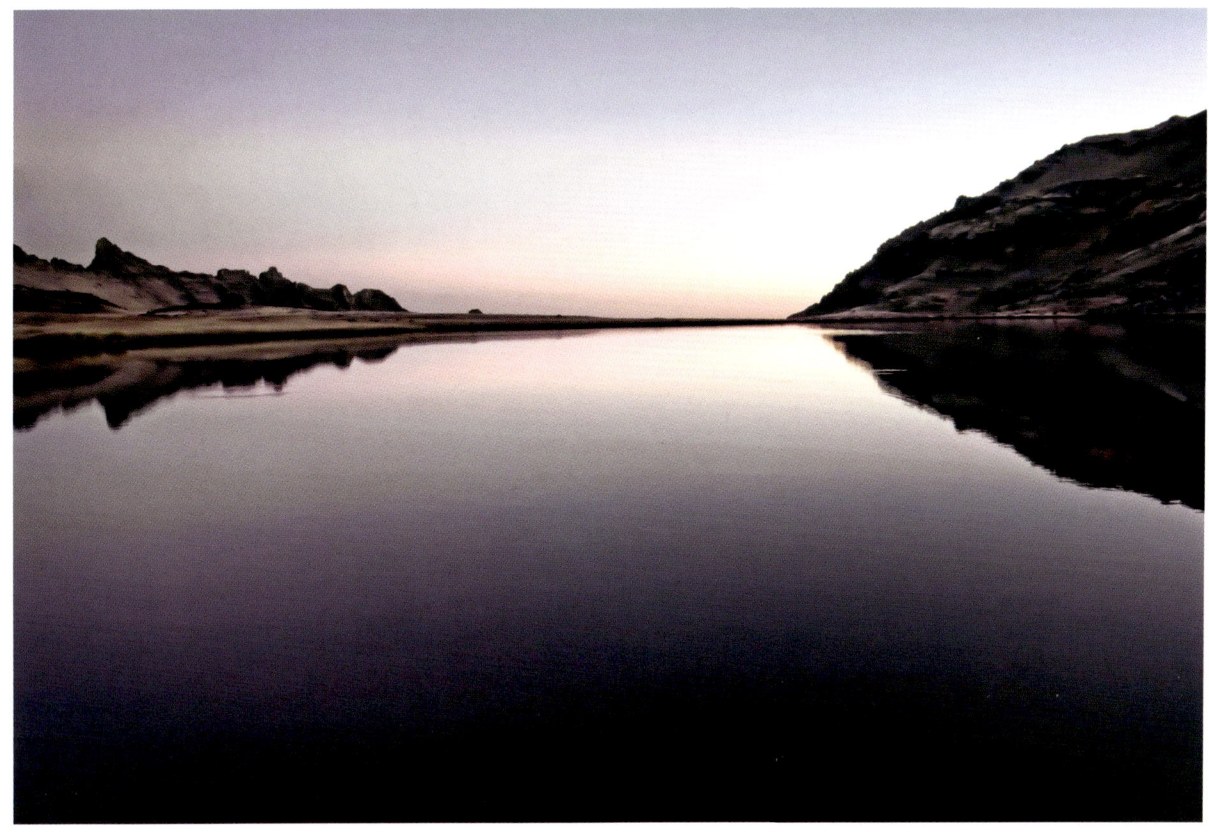

Wildhorse Lake at dawn, Steens Mountain. *Photo by Matt Witt*

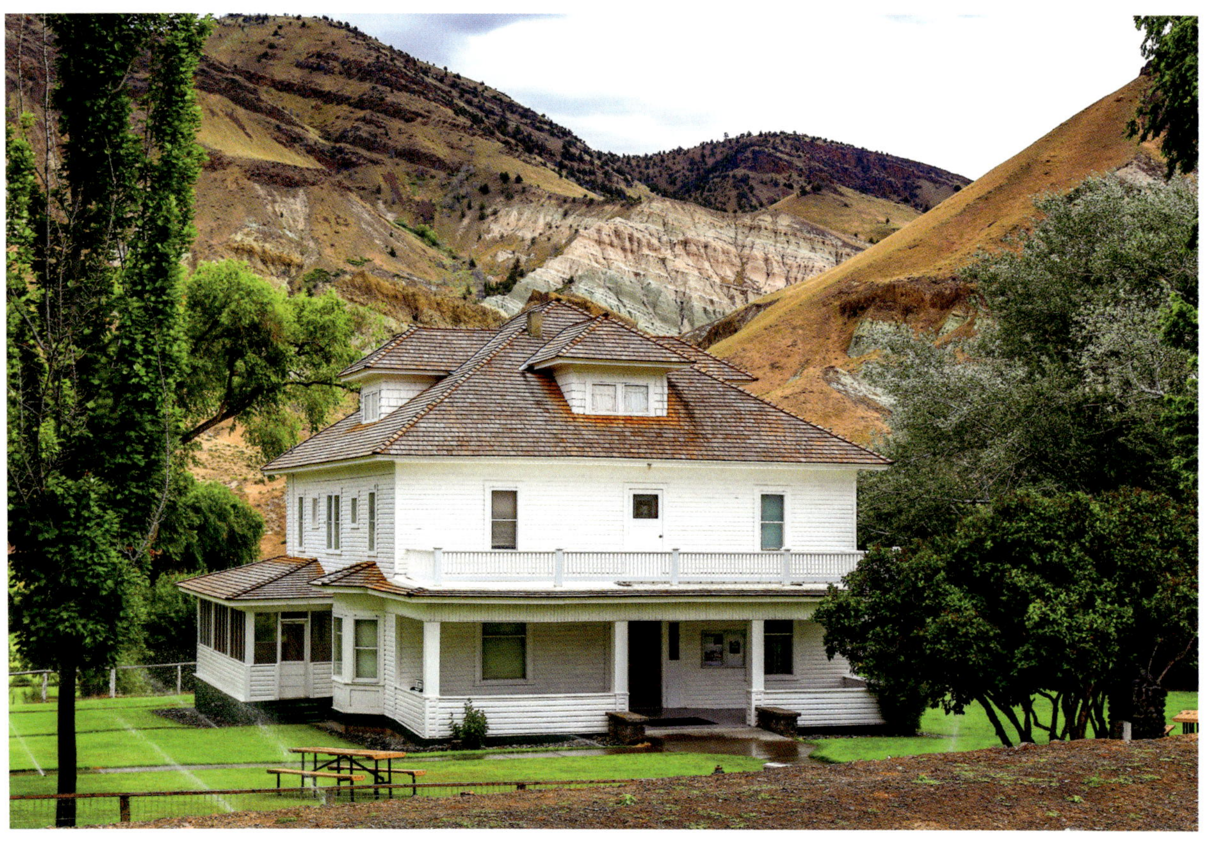

Cant Ranch, John Day Fossil Beds National Monument. The ranch, built in 1917, is the headquarters for the John Day Fossil Beds. *Photo by Terry Fisher*

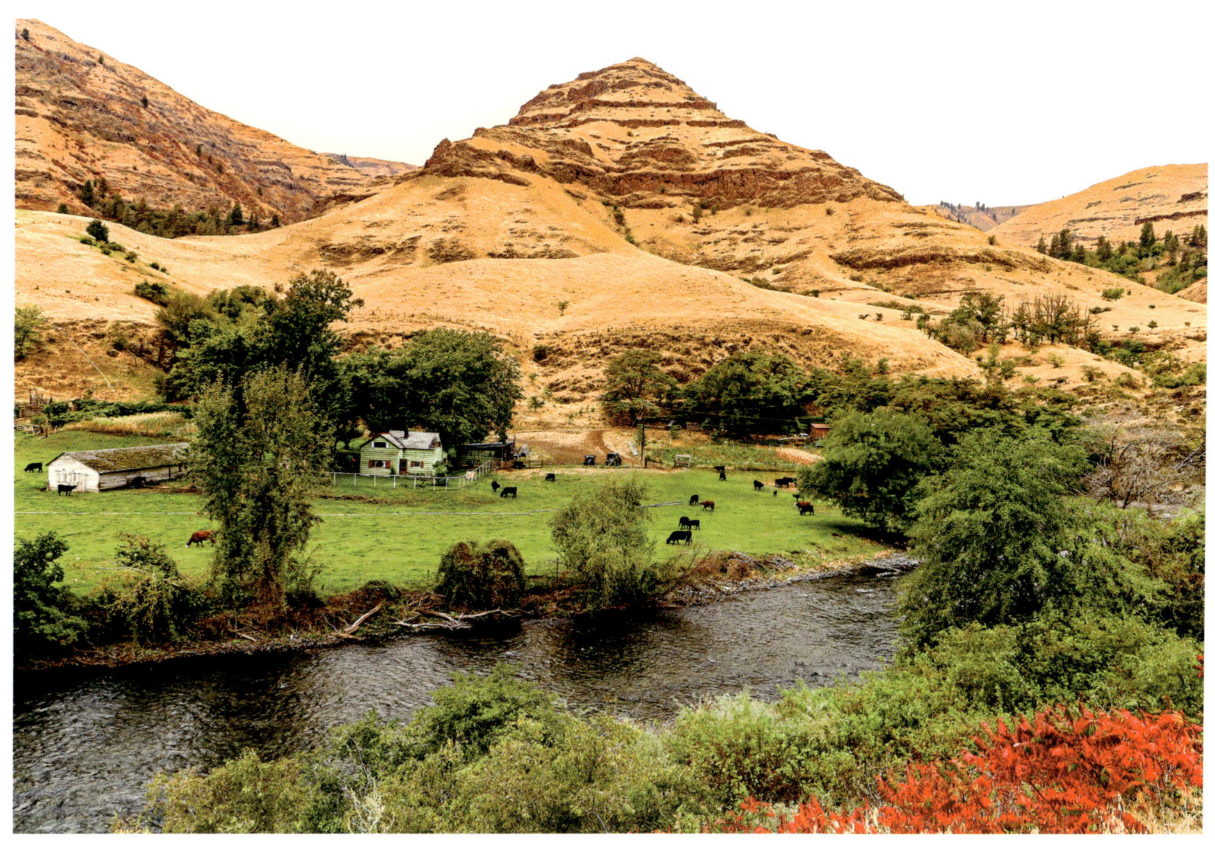

Ranch along Imnaha River. Imnaha is the easternmost settlement in Oregon. *Photo by Terry Fisher*

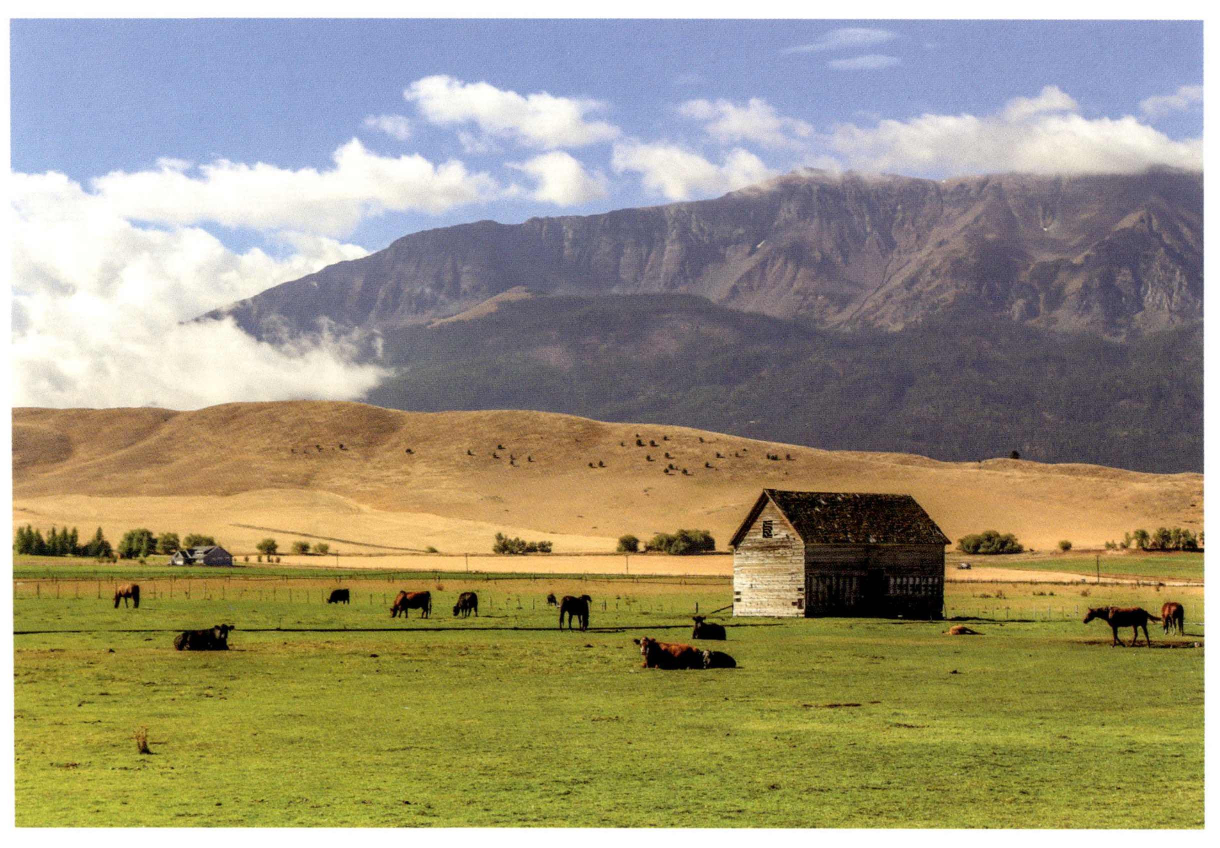

Wallowa Mountains. *Photo by Terry Fisher*

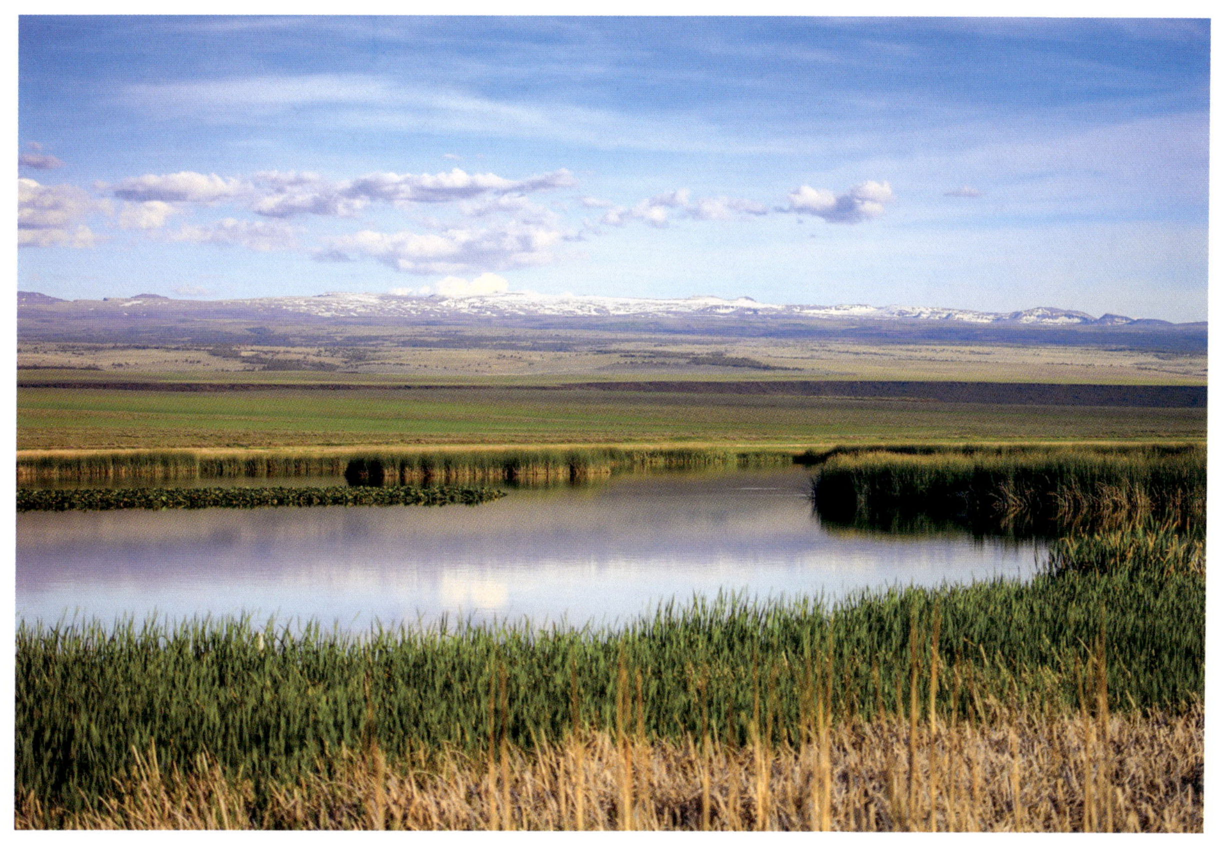

Benson Pond, Malheur National Wildlife Refuge. Steens Mountain in background. *Photo by Terry Fisher*

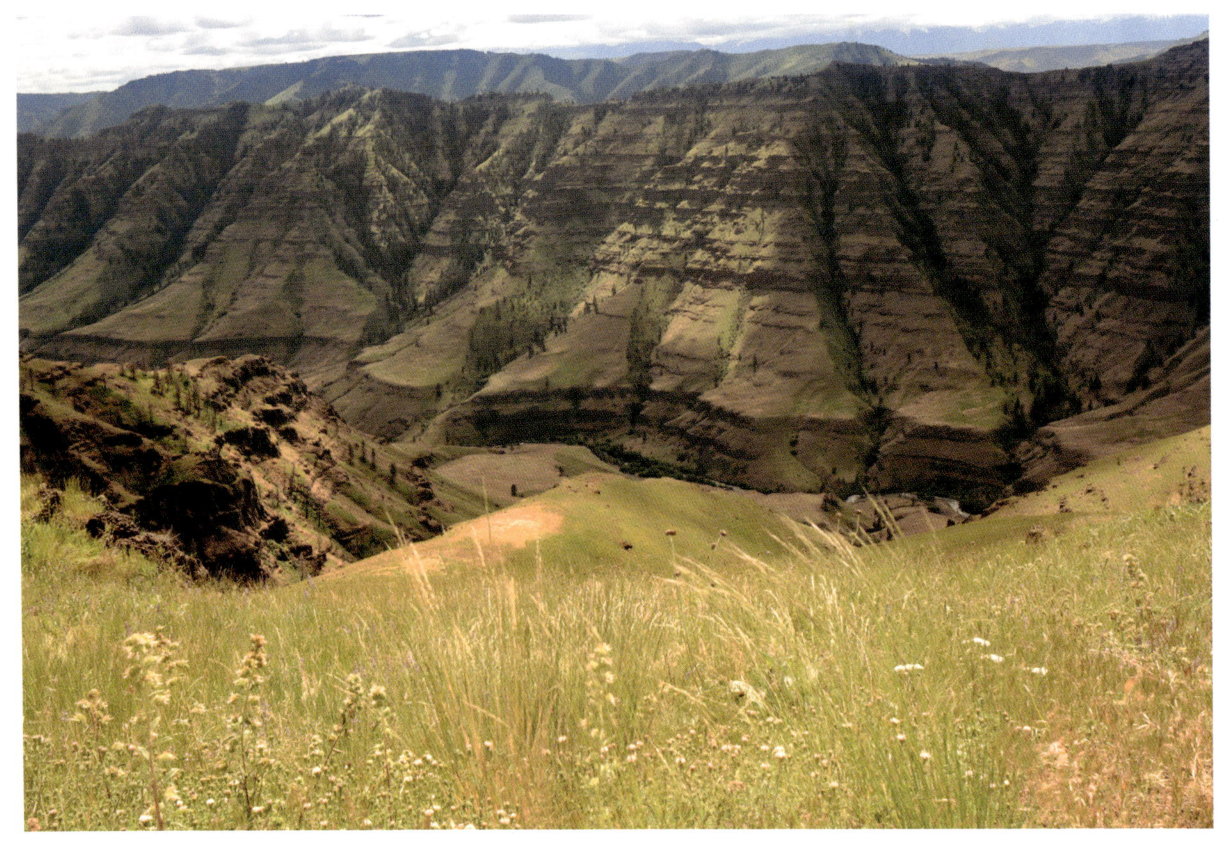

Imnaha Canyon. *Photo by Hans Stroo*

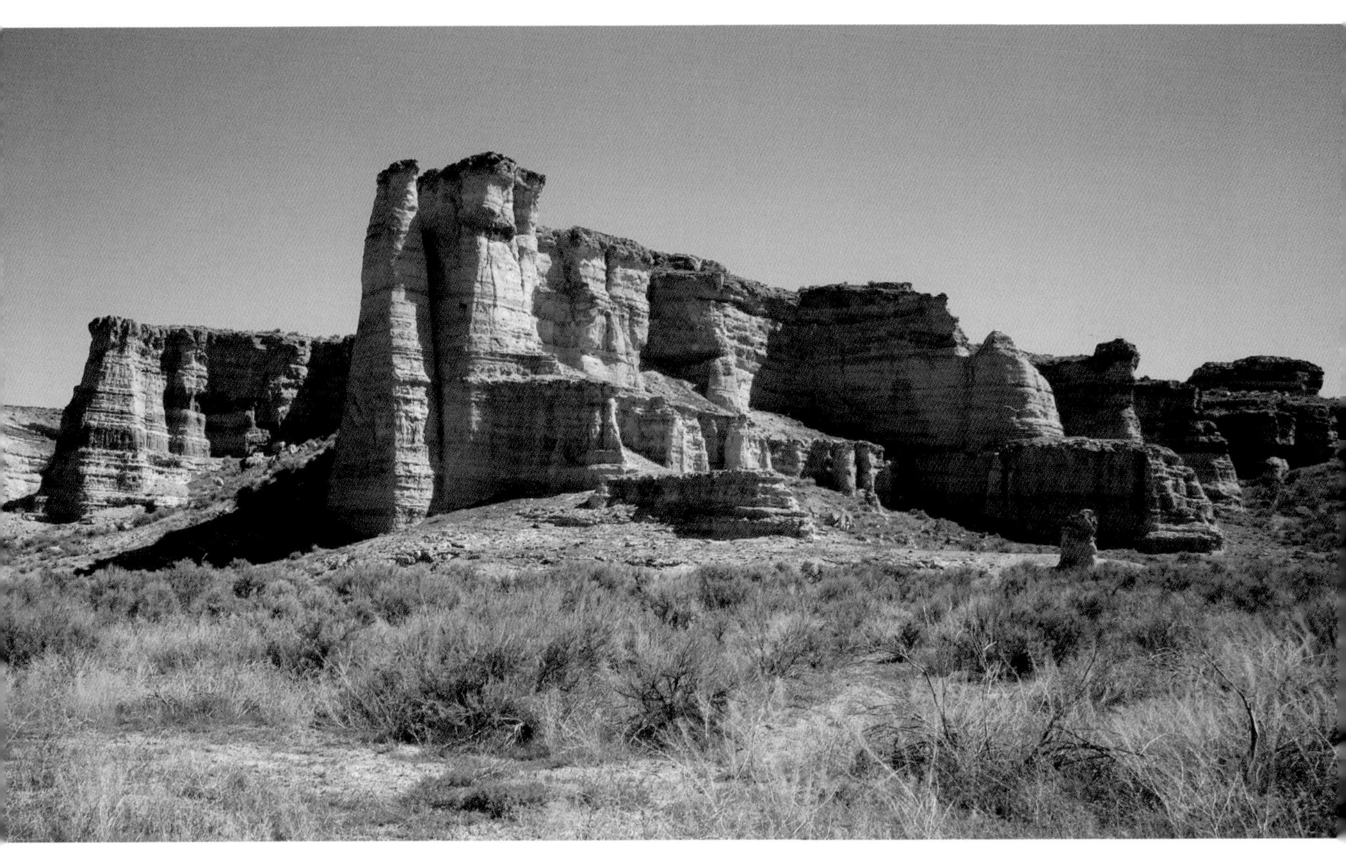

Pillars of Rome, Owyhee. These 100-foot-high formations measure about 5 miles long and 2 miles wide. *Photo by John Kirk*

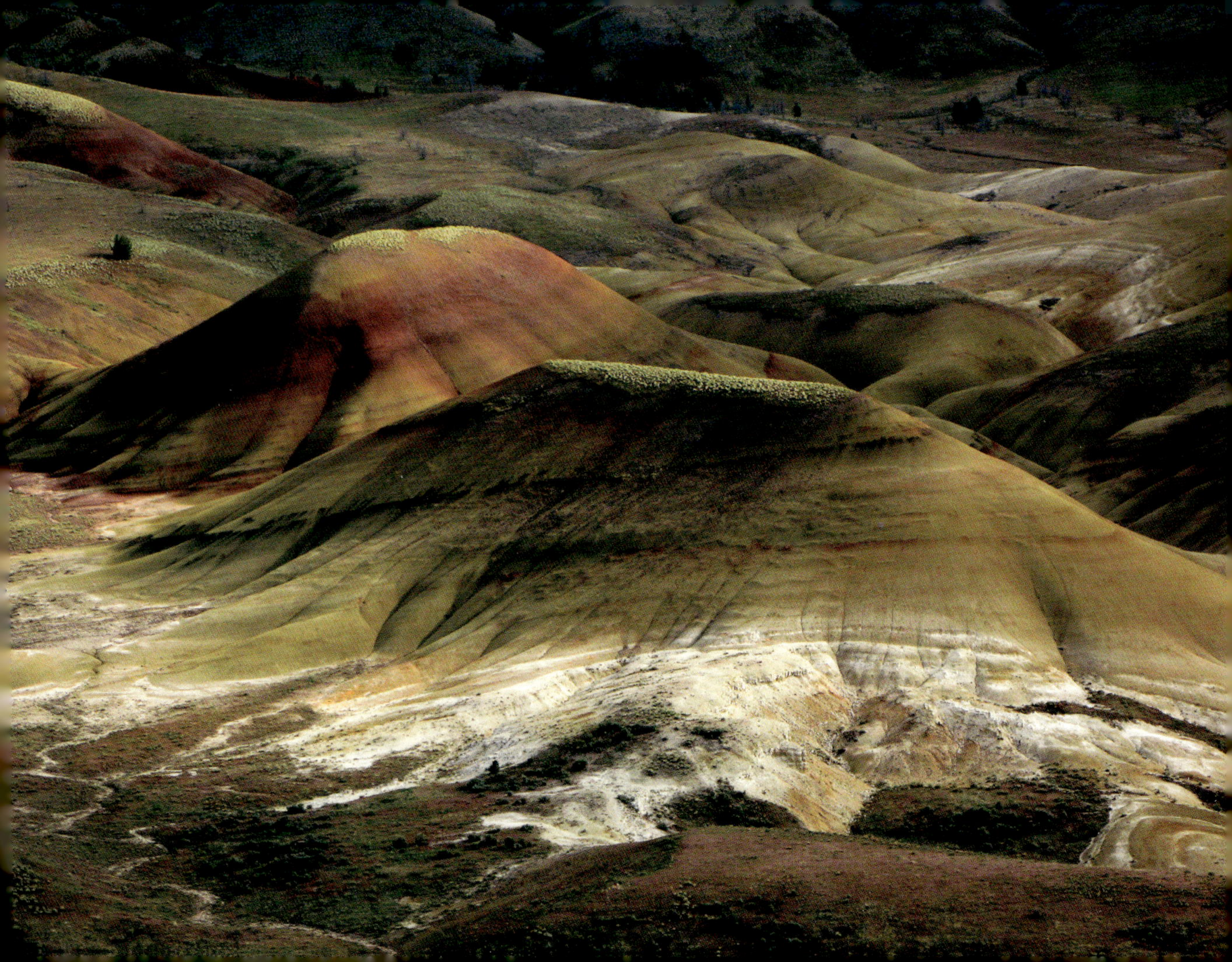

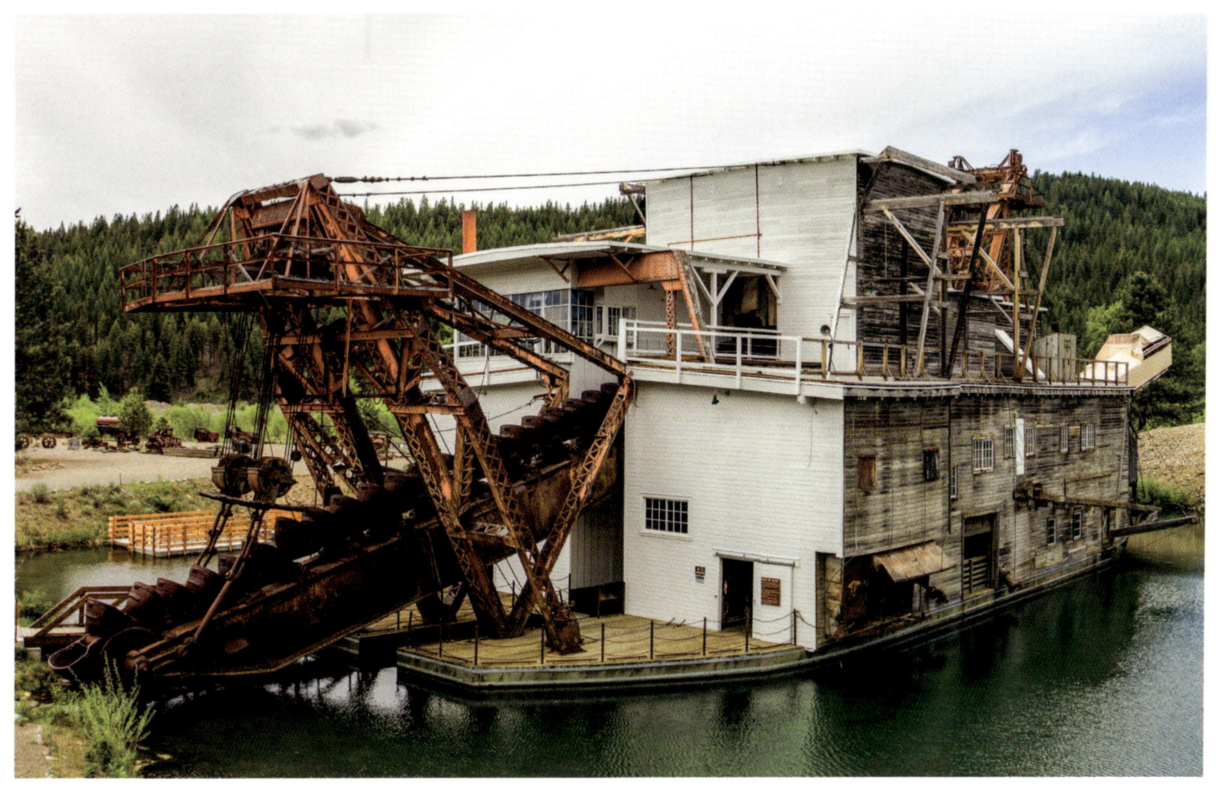

Painted Hills. *Photo by Nomeca Hartwell*

Sumpter Valley Gold Dredge. *Photo by Alan Ingersoll*

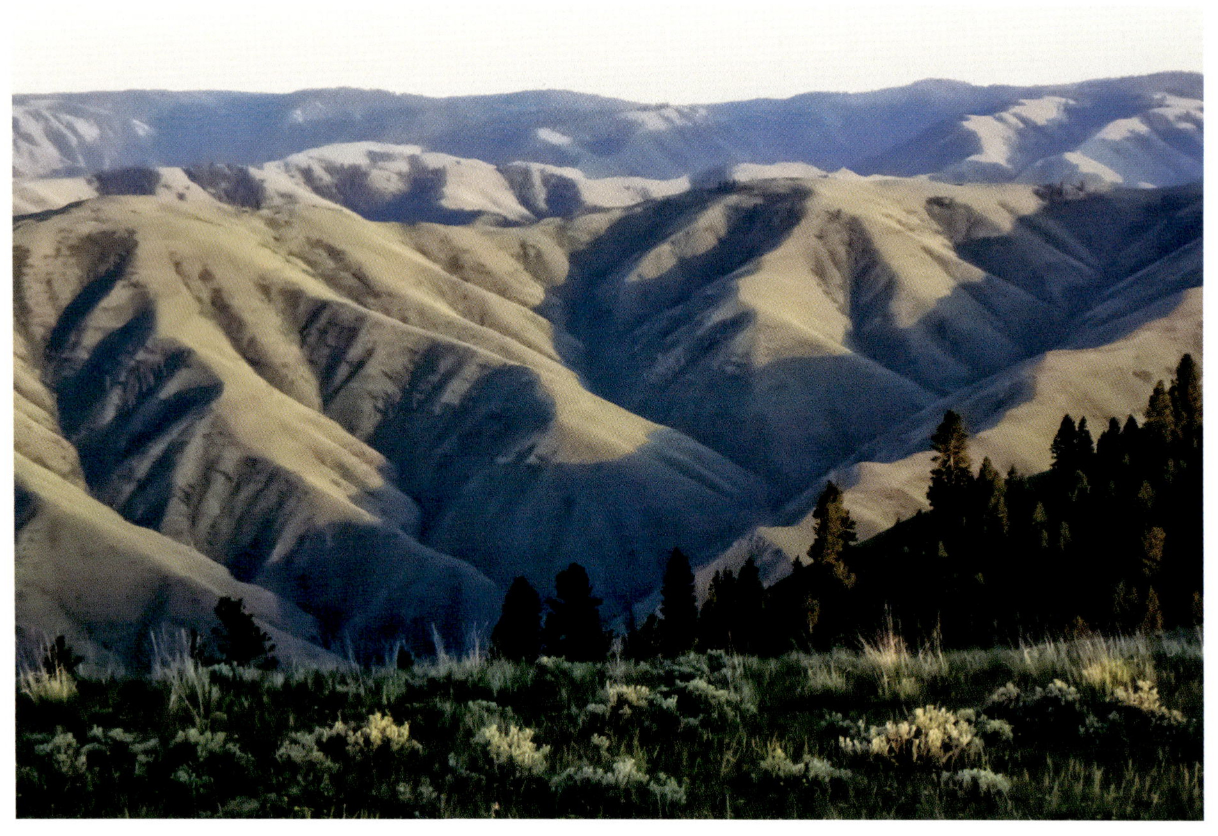

Blue Mountains. *Photo by Vivian McAleavey*

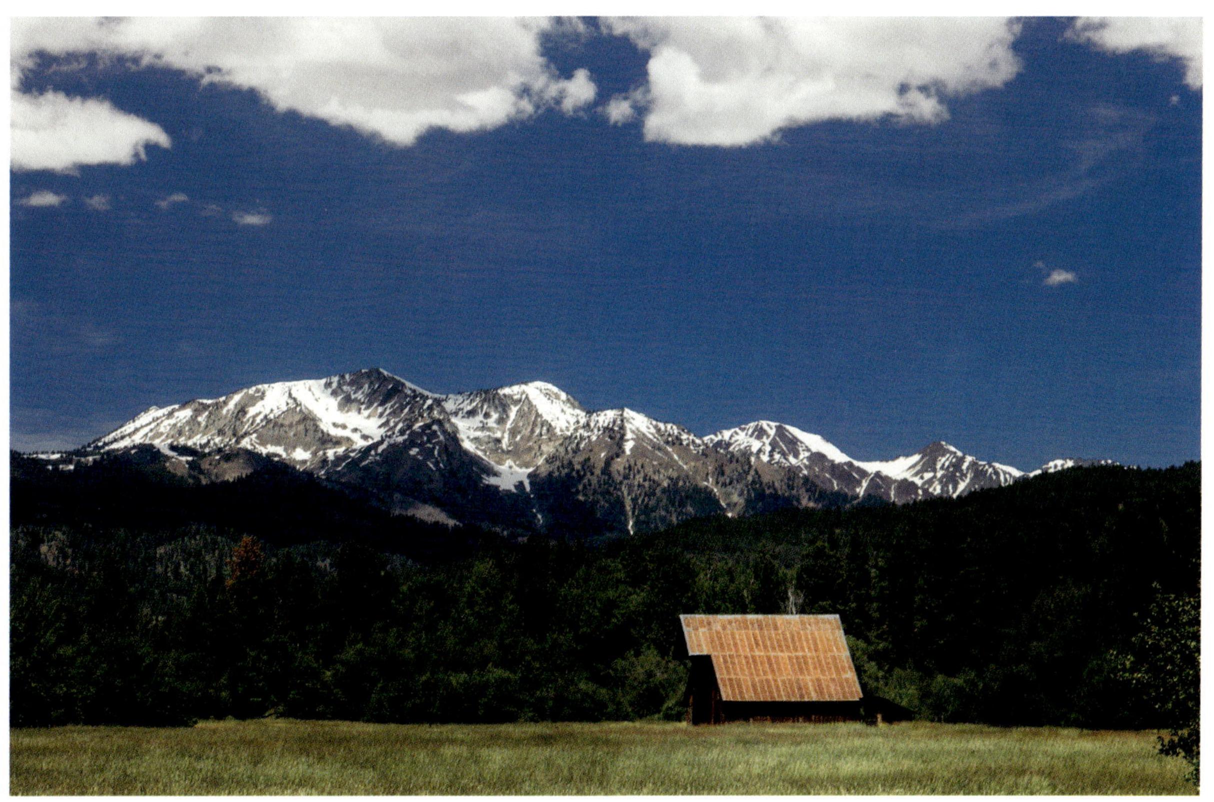

Wallowa Mountains near Halfway. *Photo by Alan Ingersoll*

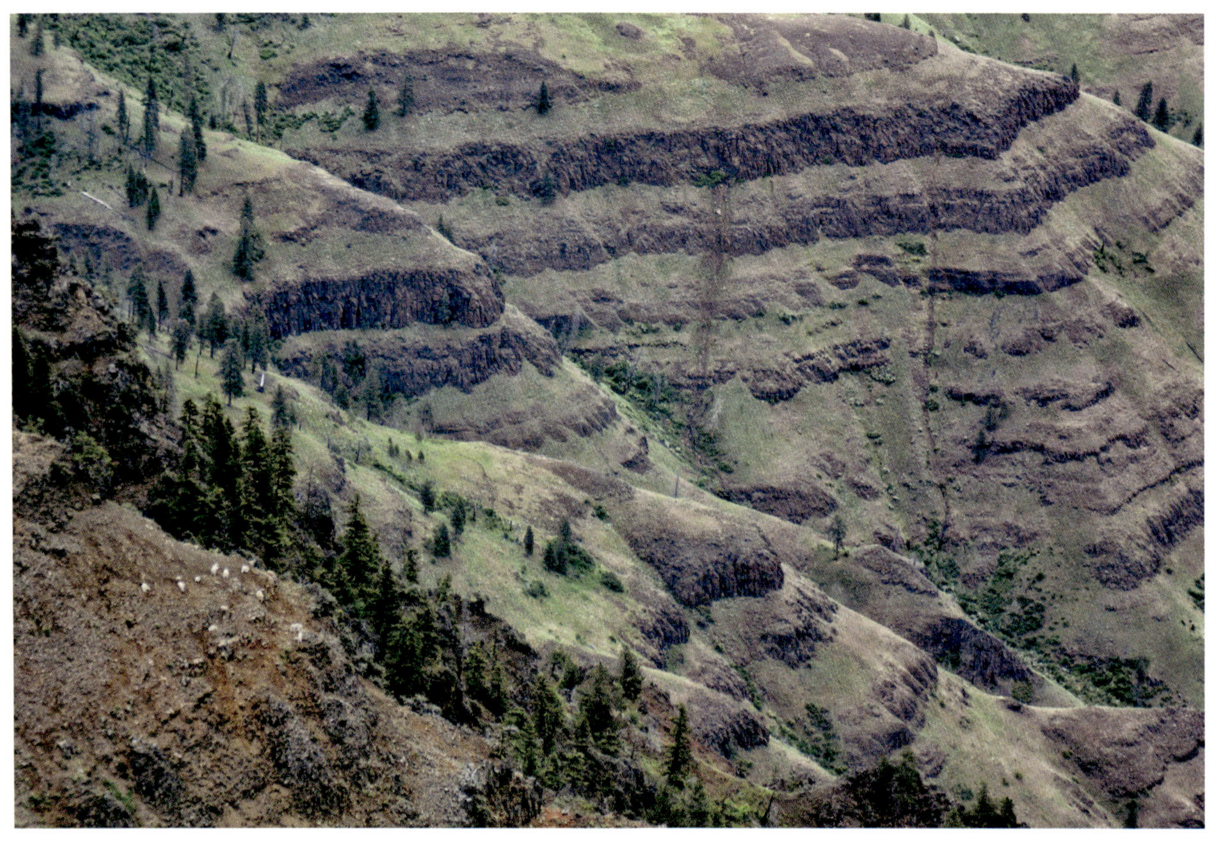

Hells Canyon and mountain goats, Wallowa Mountains. North America's deepest river gorge, and one of the deepest gorges on earth. *Photo by Hans Stroo*

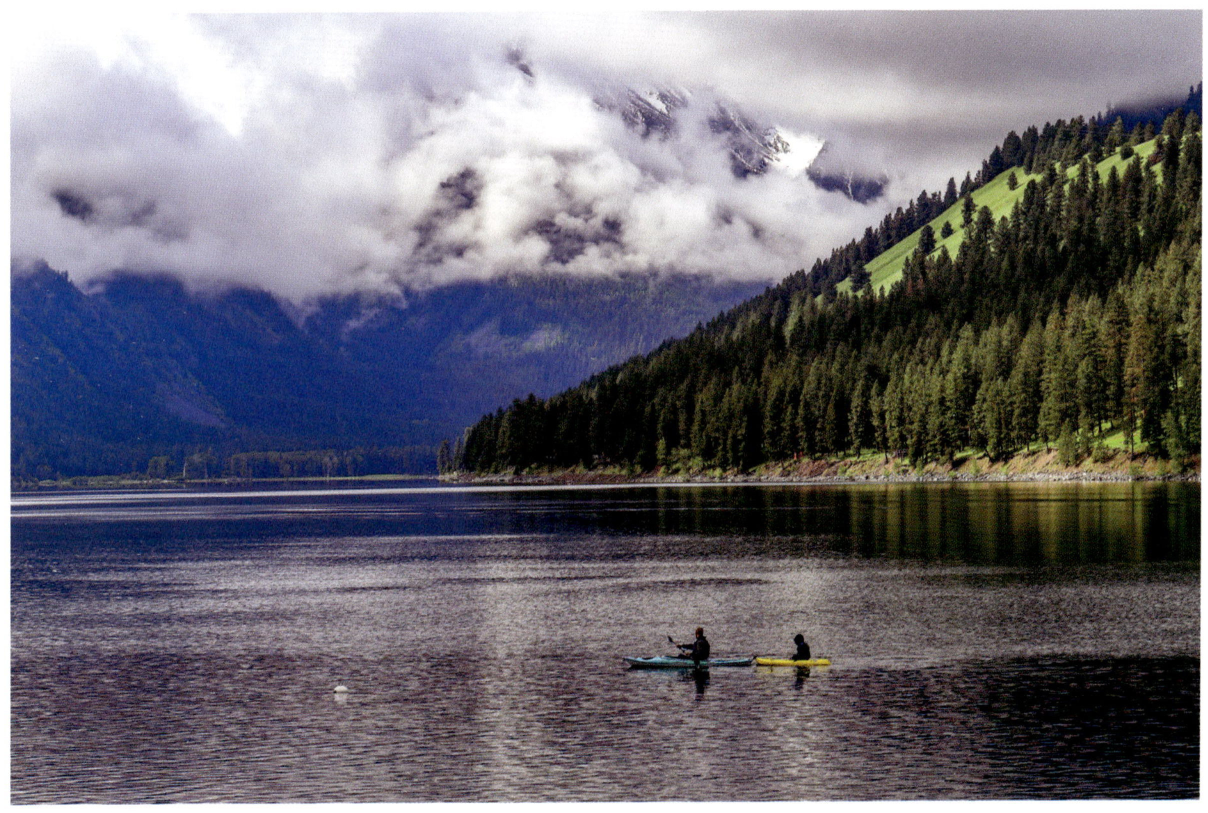

Wallowa Lake, near Chief Joseph's grave. *Photo by Terry Fisher*

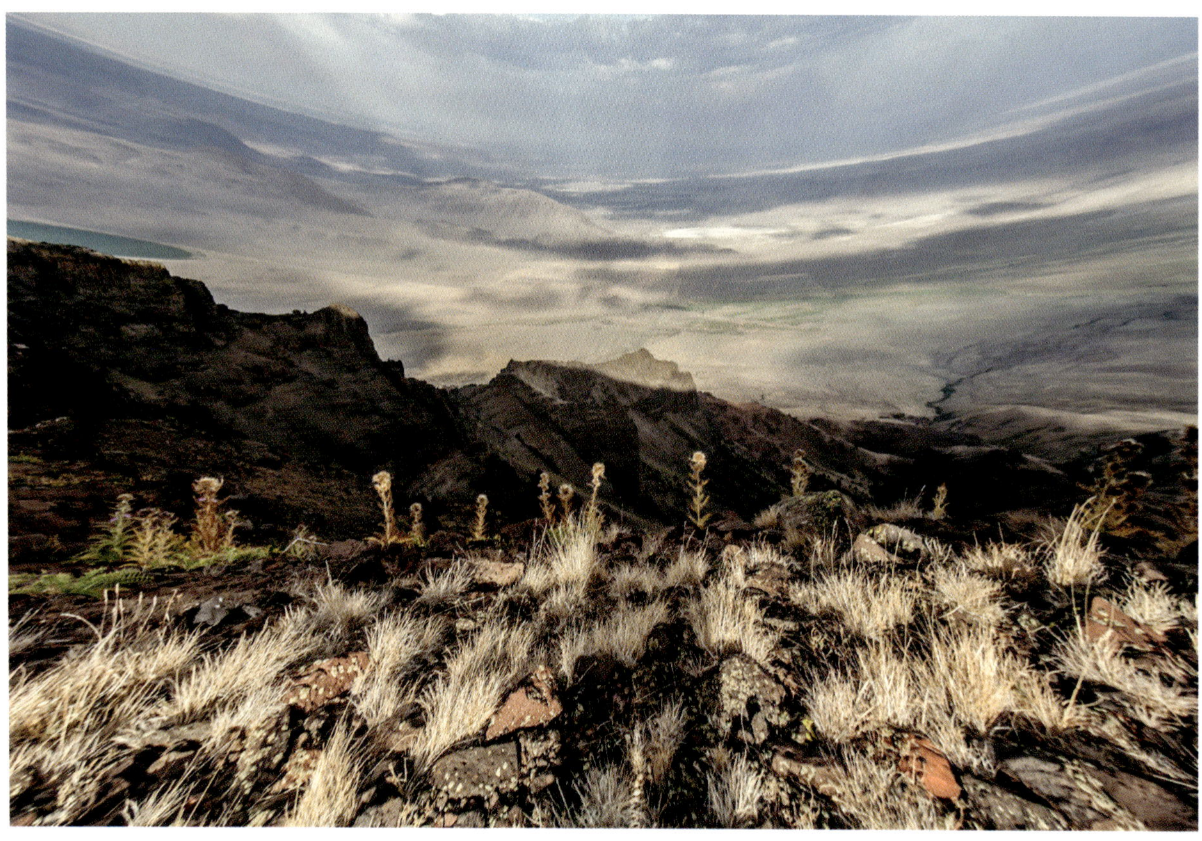

Steens Mountain. *Photo by Diana Standing*

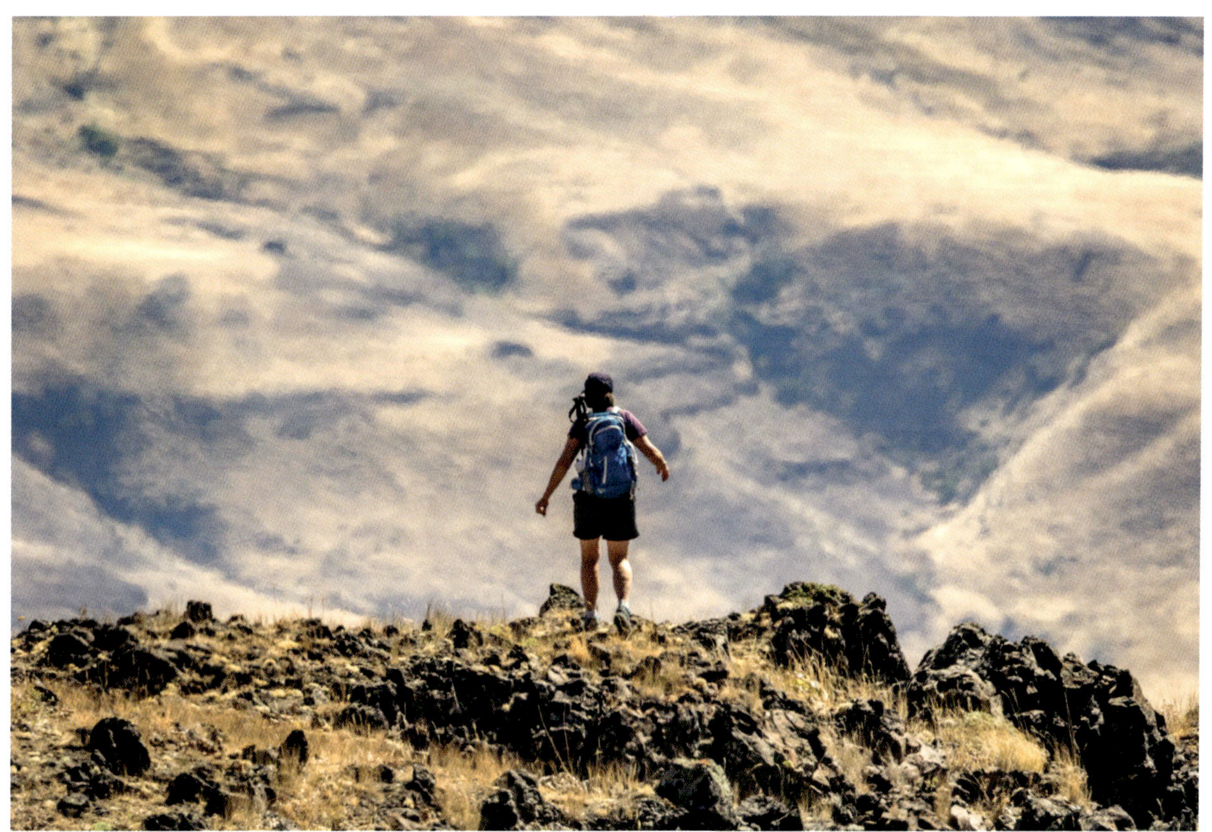

Buckhorn Overlook, Zumwalt Prairie. *Photo by Nick Viani*

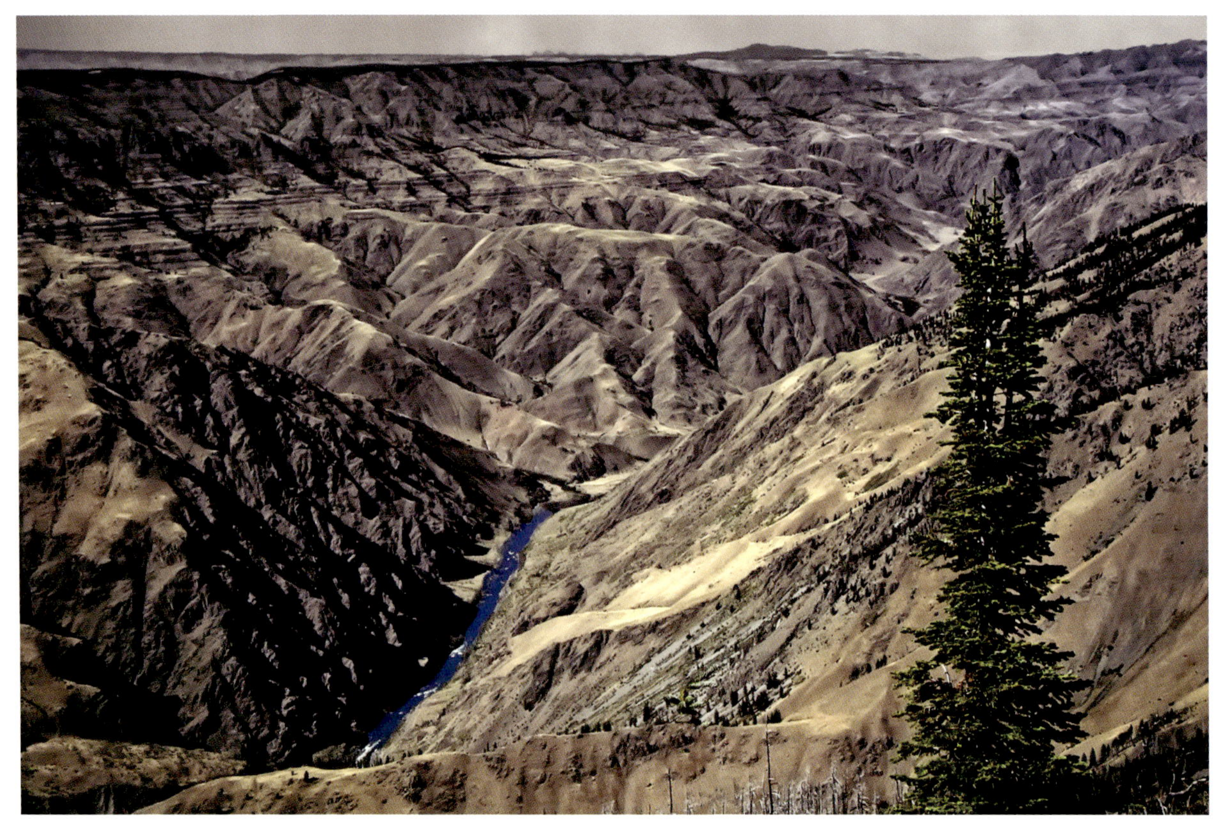

Snake River, Hells Canyon. *Photo by Matt Witt*

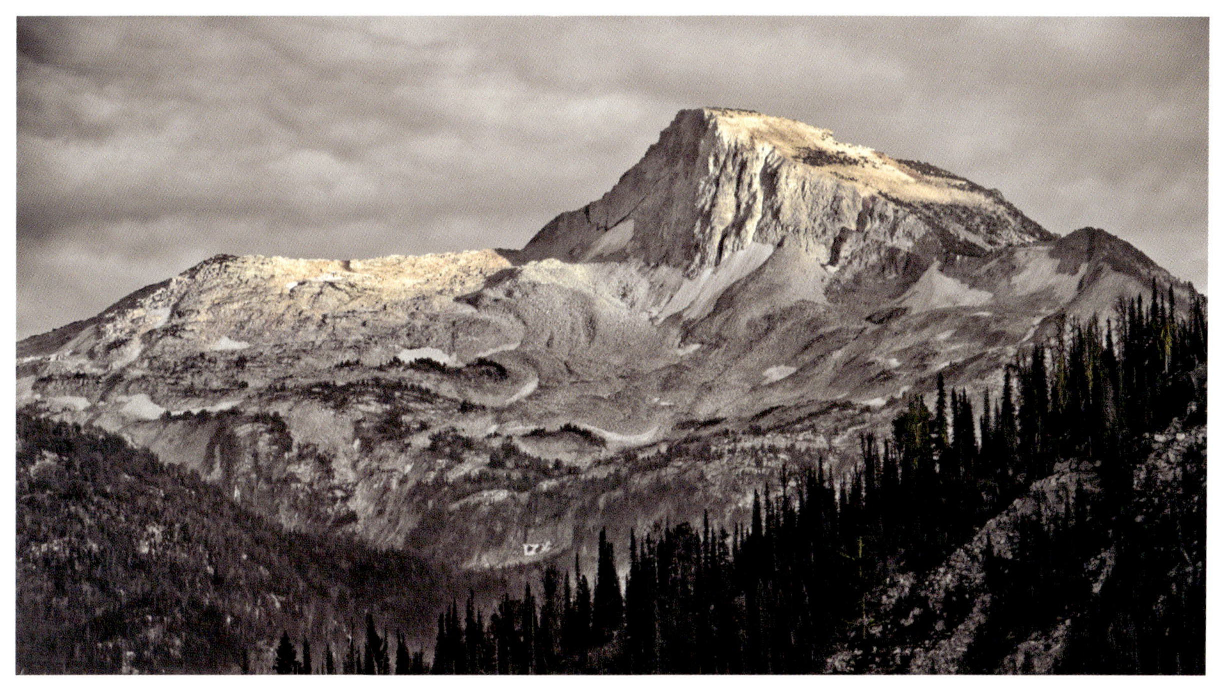

Eagle Cap, in the Wallowa Mountains range of northeast Oregon.
Photo by Matt Witt

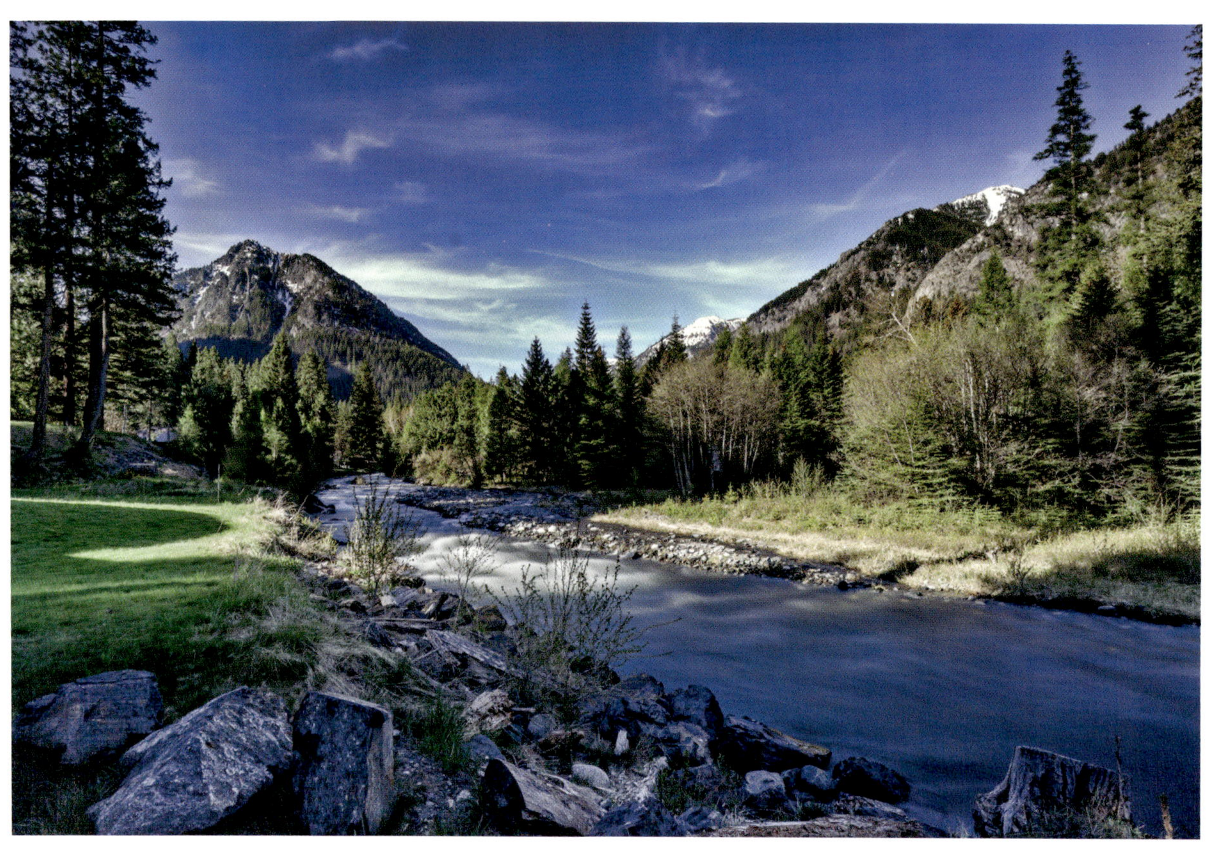

Wallowa River, near the community of Joseph. *Photo by Nick Viani*

CREDITS

Thank you to the following Oregon photographers who contributed to this book:

Randy Bryan
Dan Elster
Terry Fisher
Nomeca Hartwell
Howard Hunt
Alan Ingersoll
John Kirk
Vivian McAleavey
Jay Newman
Sue Newman
Clem Paslack
George F. Peterson
Andrea Shapiro
Diana Standing
Alana Lynn Starkweather
Hans Stroo
Vldn Taylor
Neal R. Thompson
Barbara Tricarico
Nick Viani
Matt Witt

Author photo credit:
Cornelius Matteo

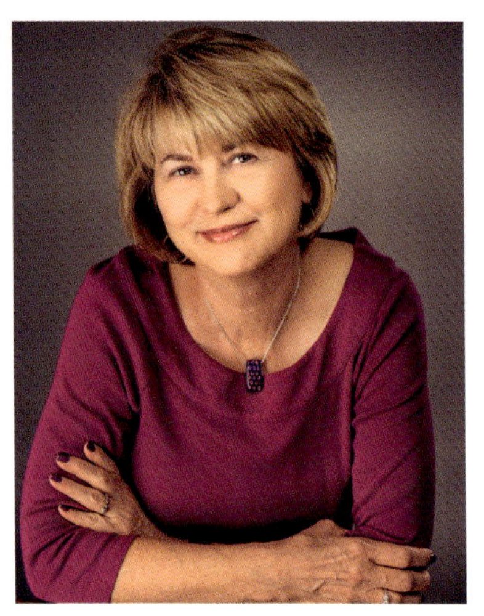

Barbara Tricarico has produced nine Oregon photography books by Schiffer, including three coffee-table books: *Oregon*; *Ashland, Oregon*; and *Ashland, Oregon Day Trips*, as well as coauthoring and photographing *Quilts of Virginia: 1607–1899*. She and her husband, Bill, moved to Ashland, Oregon, in 2010. Barbara is an active member of the Ashland Chamber of Commerce and Southern Oregon Photographic Association. She is a regular volunteer for the Ashland Food Project and the Oregon Shakespeare Festival. Barbara has traveled and photographed extensively around the world. Follow her on Facebook at Barbara Tricarico Photography or visit her website, www.barbaratricarico.com.